INFANTS, CHILDREN, AND YOUTH

María Florencia Amigó

INFANTS, CHILDREN, AND YOUTH

Multi-sited Stories of Adversity from South Asia to Australia

Cultural Anthropology

Collection Editors

Nila Ginger Hofman & Janise Hurtig

LPp

First published in 2025 by Lived Places Publishing

British Library Cataloguing in Publication Data
A CIP record for this book is available from the British Library.

ISBN: 9781916704046 (pbk)
ISBN: 9781916704060 (ePDF)
ISBN: 9781916704053 (ePUB)

Cover design by Fiachra McCarthy
Book design by Rachel Trolove of Twin Trail Design
Typeset by Newgen Publishing, UK

Lived Places Publishing
P.O. Box 1845
47 Echo Avenue
Miller Place, NY 11764

www.livedplacespublishing.com

Abstract

This book unfolds stories of transitions from infancy to adulthood across diverse cultures and adverse contexts. Each chapter explores a life stage, from birth on Simeulue Island, Indonesia, highlighting undernutrition, to migrant children in inner Sydney, Australia, navigating schooling. It moves on to working children in Lombok, Indonesia, adolescent marriage in Sunsari, Nepal, and working-class youth in Western Sydney striving for self-sufficiency. Grounded in ethnographic principles, the stories offer unique cultural perspectives and emphasise resilience and hope, advocating for an anthropology that focuses on human invincible hope rather than grim adversity.

Keywords

Anthropology of children and youth
Contexts of Adversity
Life Stages
Life Transitions
Ethnography
Multi-sited stories
Anthropology of the Good
Indonesia
Nepal
Australia

Contents

1
Introduction

Learning objectives

By the end of this chapter, students should be able to critically examine the concept of childhood, recognising that it is a socially constructed and culturally specific phenomenon rather than a universal, biological stage of life. They will understand how the notion of what it means to be a "child" is shaped by historical and geographical contexts and how the idea of childhood has been largely constructed through the lens of the "global north". Students will also explore the implications of this "universalisation" of childhood, especially in terms of its influence on global policies and practices, including those related to education, child labour, and child rights. In addition, students will develop a deeper understanding of how structural violence – such as poverty, inequality, and marginalisation – impacts children in various parts of the world, often shaping their life chances and choices, identity, and personhood.

* * * * *

Man is born free, and everywhere he is in chains

Jean-Jacques Rousseau (1762)

This is a book for those interested in the diverse pathways that take us through the transition into "adulthood" and in the variety of experiences, circumstances, and interactions that can accompany that journey. This is a book made of real stories, from diverse settings, that intends to expand our **emotional** understanding of what it takes to go through infancy, childhood, and youth to become an "adult", or an individual that can finally be acknowledged as a fully formed, socialised, and independent member of a community. As a discipline that has at its core the desire to find out what makes us human and what is common and different across humankind, anthropology offers the right approach for this project.

Anthropologists have long been fascinated by cross-cultural appraisals of the lived experiences of infants, children, and youth (e.g., Lancy, 2008; Montgomery, 2009). In the last three decades, the anthropology of childhood has gained momentum, especially as a way of contesting globalising ideas of who children are and how their lives ought to be governed (e.g., Cregan and Cuthbert, 2014). The study of childhood has advanced significantly, enabling new critical understandings and robust theoretical frameworks, reinforcing the notion that "infancy", "childhood", and "youth" are not universal categories but cultural constructions, while also reminding us of the broad variation in children's physical, cognitive, and emotional development and of the role of context in shaping these dynamics (e.g., Lavine and New, 2008). These critical approaches to the study of "childhood" have helped us challenge "one size fits all" pronouncements and regulations around children's lives — such as when a child can or should work, become sexually active, get married, start and finish formal schooling, have a child, or participate in armed conflict — as these can be oblivious to engrained cultural norms and power dynamics brought about by gender, race, ethnicity, and social status, making essentialist/universalist pronouncements or regulations not only inadequate but also unrealistic (e.g., Cregan and Cuthbert, 2014). Stephens (1995) put this very compellingly in her discussion of what she refers to as "the luxury of childhood", meaning that discourses around the preciousness of children, and thus how their lives should be governed, are the result of the "exportation" of a historically recent idea of childhood in the "global North"[1], of which the 1990 UN Convention on the Rights of the Child is an example. Other seminal works (Liebel, 2020; Cannella and Viruru, 2004) have focused on the role of colonial histories and their legacy in generating not only deep inequalities in young lives across the world but also political and educational practices that, instead of redressing these inequalities, end up reproducing them.

The stories in this book are written within this scholarly context and reinforce the ethnographic reality around how the lives of many infants, children, and youth on the planet diverge significantly from dominant, media-bloated discourses on how humans should progress through life, from the time of birth until we become independent from our primary carers. Humans are the only species that requires intense and extensive parental care – the closest example would be chimpanzees, who parent their offspring for about seven years. The chapters that follow point at the truly diverse way in which human offspring are assisted in their journey into "adulthood" or rather into "self-sufficiency". Whether these diverse ways are ideal or not is for the reader to assess, but what is clear is that, in their path to self-sufficiency, offspring and those who care for them need to juggle various contextual factors.

Much of the academic knowledge that stipulates what ought to be optimal physical, cognitive, and emotional development; ideal schooling patterns; preferred ways of relating to parents, teachers, friends, or employers; or the best age to become financially independent or get married may be based on robust scholarly evidence as well as noble intentions, but may not consider that for these optimal outcomes, specific contextual factors would also be needed. And because humans live and operate in a complex mesh of cultural norms, varied material conditions, and distinct political landscapes, what may be optimal in terms of human development can often be unfeasible. The stories in this book are about the unfolding of young lives in contexts that are real and often challenging, that is, contexts of adversity.

Shaped by adversity, resisting adversity

Anthropologist and physician Paul Farmer uses the sociological term "structural violence" (2004) to refer to a form of violence that is embedded in the social, political, and economic structures of society, resulting from unequal access to resources, opportunities, and basic rights. Unlike common forms of violence involving direct physical or mental harm, structural violence indirectly leads to disparities and inequalities in access to education, housing, healthcare, or employment.

The stories in this book take place in adverse environments linked to diverse forms of structural violence. The geographies, institutions, and social relationships within the localities where the storytellers in this book live are harsh. Be it due to restricted access to resources, environmentally sound environments, employment, education, or healthcare, or due to human norms and relationships that limit the autonomy of individuals, these contexts where infants, children, and youth unfold their lives turn into hostile forces that in turn shape particular personhoods.

This book, however, aims not to perpetuate a grim and pessimistic tone often found in scholarly works influenced by the critical social sciences. While acknowledging the inequalities and injustices prevalent in the settings of these stories, the following chapters seek to illuminate how infants, children, and youth in these circumstances resist adversity. They strive to survive, learn, support their families' progress, experience love, find partners, have children of their own, and secure decently paid work. Adversity is undeniably real for them, yet it serves as a crucible that fuels their hope, refining and fortifying their character, beliefs, and resilience. Despite facing disadvantages in the "unequal distribution of hope" (Hage, 2003), the young lives showcased in this book – together with their caregivers and educators— are engaged in choosing what they believe are the best nutrients and care for their babies, in adjusting to schooling systems that teach them in unfamiliar languages, or in fighting against the poverty that threatens their families' survival, contesting rigid societal norms that dictate their marriage choices, or dismissing exploitative employers who seek cheap labour and offer only disrespect and precarious working conditions.

(Dis) Connected ethnographies of infants, children, and youth

The chapters that follow are deliberately organised following the sequence in the life span of the early stages of the life of a human being, from birth to the early twenties when almost anywhere young adults are expected to be now self-sufficient. Each of the chapters contains a handful of stories stemming from a single ethnographic project that revolved around a particular theme. Some of the chapters (Chapters 3 and 4) report on academic projects, while others are derived from commissioned research (Chapters 2, 5, and 6). However, ethnographic principles underpin the ways in which *all* the stories were collected, interpreted, and rewritten. In ethnography, the researcher deliberatively intends to establish a connection with the storytellers, be mindful of the histories that have shaped their environments, and, whenever possible, strive to understand their realities from their unique cultures and perspectives. In most cases, I collected the stories directly, while a handful were collected by research assistants – individuals who were from the same culture being studied. But without exception, the stories in this book draw from ethnography not just as a research tool but as an ethical principle that helps bring humans from diverse contexts and cultures together by enabling transformative mutual understandings (Behar, 1996; Das 2007; Valle, 2016).

Multi-sited stories

Because the stories in this book were gathered at various points in time, by different story-collectors, and in diverse localities, the reader will note that each chapter offers a particular narrative style. For instance, Chapter 4 includes the voice of the first person, where the author integrates into the narrative, as the stories stem from a long period of fieldwork. The styles in other chapters range from offering more intimate narratives with some of the storytellers — for instance, when the author was interviewing them in Spanish, her native language (Chapter 3)—to adopting a more observational stance when the conversations took place online as they happened during the pandemic (Chapter 6) or when extracting narratives gleaned from story-collectors who, under the guidance of the author, spoke the language of those sharing their accounts (Chapters 2 and 5). This diversity in style reflects the multi-sited nature of the stories, which also echoes the variety of human experiences around growing up and developing as a human being. The terminology to refer to different stages of a human's development is rooted in concepts that will be familiar to most readers. Although the terms "baby", "toddler", "child", "adolescent", "teenager", and "youth" or "young person" are also culturally and historically specific, these are used loosely throughout the book to refer to the chronologically equivalent stages in the non-Western contexts of Simeulue, Indonesia (Chapter 2), Lombok, Indonesia (Chapter 4), and Sunsari, Nepal (Chapter 5). Also, in keeping with ethnographic writing (e.g., Van Maanen, 2011), occasionally vernacular terms are used where they can better convey an idea or concept.

Although all the multi-sited stories in this book are about babies, children, and young individuals, these individuals are not always able to speak for themselves. Clearly, during the early stages of life, language is undeveloped, or developing; therefore, those in close contact with children (such as guardians or educators) are best placed to interpret their lives. For this reason, in Chapters 2 and 3, it is mothers, fathers, nurses, teachers, or other relevant community members who report on the adversities that revolve around the young lives they are responsible for.

Contour lines

Although each chapter is self-contained and can be read in isolation, my intention as an author is for the reader to find how one chapter leads to the following one, if only as a way of tracing the evolution of a new life and the different fronts against which that life must fight, in the contexts of nutrition and physical care, language and basic education, economic contribution to the family unit, coming of age and mating, and getting paid for work to achieve financial independence. Despite the geographically distant and culturally distinct contexts in which the stories are located, the young lives within them may be subject to forces that are relatable to each other.

Critical geographer Cindi Katz (2001) extends the geographical concept of topography to refer to how landscapes are not just characterised by physical features (such as their terrain) but also by the social and cultural dimensions of that particular space. In this sense, topography serves as a framework to examine how physical spaces are not neutral but also **lived** places (see also de Certeau, 1980). Her concept of "countertopography" aims to uncover the human complexities that exist within seemingly neutral landscapes, and she uses the metaphor of "contour lines" to convey how distant physical spaces are interconnected through similar social, economic, and political processes. My aim is for the reader to draw mental contour lines that traverse and link each of the stories in this book, and in doing so identify how the uniqueness of human experiences often reveals shared aspects of our collective existence. My aim is also for readers to consider how **emotions**, as a fundamental common feature of our humanity, connect us with others and become instrumental in our efforts to survive, thrive, and leave descendants, no matter where we are situated.

* * * * *

Extension activities

To extend their learning, students will engage in a series of activities aimed at deepening their understanding of the complexities impacting infants, children, and youth in different cultural contexts.

Extension Activity 1: Students will research and present case studies on how the concept of childhood differs across various cultures, focusing on a specific region or community. They will be tasked with identifying key cultural practices, rites of passage, and societal expectations that shape childhood experiences in their chosen context.

Extension Activity 2: In small groups, students will examine a real-world issue related to childhood (e.g., child labour, education inequalities, child marriage) in a global context, using an anthropological lens to analyse the structural violence at play. They will present their findings, drawing connections between cultural norms, global policies, and the lived realities of children.

Extension Activity 3: Students will participate in a debate on whether the global "rights-based" approach to childhood, as advocated by organisations like the United Nations Children's Fund (UNICEF), successfully addresses or oversimplifies the diverse realities faced by children worldwide. This will help students critically evaluate the tension between universal norms and cultural diversity in shaping childhood experiences and policies.

2
Nutrition. Resilience: Born in Aceh, Indonesia

Learning objectives

By the end of this chapter, students should be able to understand the complex factors contributing to the nutrition and care of infants aged 0–5 years, particularly in the context of poverty and limited access to resources. Students will explore the interplay between traditional beliefs around food and child-rearing practices, and the challenges faced in integrating medically validated health information into local practices. They will critically analyse the role of family and extended family in shaping children's health outcomes, recognising that survival in impoverished contexts often hinges on local knowledge and community support. Additionally, students will gain an understanding of the barriers to healthcare access, including issues of trust in healthcare providers, and how these may affect the health and well-being of young children. Students will also be encouraged to think about the developmental consequences of malnutrition and the broader social and cultural factors that influence the adoption of health advice.

* * * * *

The first five years of life are the building blocks for any individual. During this period, the brain blossoms and overall health takes root. Physical, cognitive, and emotional growth during this stage determine prospects in life. The recipe for optimising this potential appears to be simple — nutritious food (including the magic of breastfeeding), a clean and safe living space with some basic sanitation infrastructure, and, very importantly, love and care. These ingredients form the bedrock for an infant's promising future.

In many corners of the world, however, this apparently simple formula, does not work. In settings shaped by economic hardships, entrenched beliefs and traditions, distrust of needy public health systems, and imbalanced power dynamics within households and communities, new lives can be caught in the middle. This chapter will zoom into the first years of children's lives in a location in the province of Aceh, Indonesia, where the nutrition and care infants receive is adversely influenced by the sociocultural environments where they live – humble and often lacking basic infrastructure, but also shaped by beliefs that are hard to uproot.

Aceh is a province nestled at the northern tip of the island of Sumatra in Northern Indonesia. Fringed by the Indian Ocean to the west and the Malacca Strait to the north, the province is known for its history of resistance, both against the exploitative Dutch colonial rule in the nineteenth century through the Aceh War (1873–1914), and against the Indonesian government from the late 1970s. The latter, which evolved into an armed conflict led by the Free Aceh Movement (GAM) to seek independence, peaked in the 1990s causing significant suffering, casualties, and human rights abuses. The conflict culminated in a peace agreement in 2005, granting Aceh a unique degree of autonomy and allowing the implementation of Sharia law – Islamic principles that govern personal conduct and community affairs. The province also garnered international attention due to the devastating impact of the 2004 Indian Ocean tsunami, which killed around 170,000 people.

In this setting, undernutrition emerges as the leading cause of disease and death in children under five. Stunting is an indicator of a child's suboptimal growth; it is based on a weak relationship between height and age, and is considered a sign of chronic undernutrition and thus compromises physical, cognitive, and emotional development. Protective factors against stunting include the mother's health during conception and pregnancy (as it influences the birthweight and overall health of the baby), exclusive breastfeeding during the first six months of life, high-quality and varied solid foods after the first six months, and good sanitation practices related to water and hygiene to prevent infections. Timely vaccination to build children's immunity and strong emotional support for the child also play a pivotal role in infants' overall well-being and growth.

In Aceh, stunting figures remain among the highest in the country, with **severe** stunting in children under five (at almost 20 per cent) leading the table in recent health censuses (see Ayuningtyas *et al.*, 2022). These stubborn figures cause curiosity as to why, in a land of abundant natural resources, good coverage of a public education system, and an extensive network of child and maternal public health posts (**Posyandu**) supported by dedicated female community volunteers known as **kaders**, young children are so prone to a vulnerable start to life.

To delve into this question, this chapter investigates the Acehnese district of Simeulue, an island with some of the highest stunting rates in the province. It draws from an ethnographic exploration of stunting in Aceh in which mothers, fathers, grandparents, health practitioners, village and religious leaders shared their knowledge on child rearing. This was part of a broader, UNICEF-funded project aimed at expanding insights into what lies behind the stubborn stunting figures, by getting a better grasp on how babies and little children are looked after by their families and public health systems from the time they are conceived.

Navigating tradition: Cultural beliefs on infant development in Simeulue

Nestled in the far Northwest of the Indonesian archipelago, Simeulue stands as a tranquil island of about 100 km long in the Indian Ocean, off the western coast of Sumatra. With a land area of 1,900 km^2 and a population of around 95,000 people, Simeulue's major town on the Southeastern coast, Sinabang, boasts about 20,000 people, with most of the island's population being rural and spread along the hillsides. Working life on Simeulue revolves around fishing, labouring on plantations (rice, coffee, tea, and coconut), and small store operations. The island's past remains enigmatic, with its history passed down through oral traditions. The Dutch, Chinese, Japanese, and mainland Acehnese have all left their imprints on Simeulue's culture and economy. In particular, mainland Acehnese – many of whom arrived during the clove boom in the 1970s and 1980s –significantly influenced the island's way of life, through Islam and the application of Aceh's Shariah law. However, indigenous communities still retain some animistic beliefs and rely on traditional values and knowledge. Political power is distributed from local village leaders to the island's governing body. Simeulue received some attention over the past two decades due to the frequent seismic activities, including earthquakes and tsunamis, which enabled the island to receive support from humanitarian organisations, and thus undergo some modernisation, with the island now benefiting from an operational airport, an expanded road network, and an extended electrical grid. However, conditions on the island remain precarious, with its healthcare and education systems still significantly underdeveloped.

Simeulue's maternal and child health services, as for the rest of Indonesia, relies on the **Posyandu** network. The **Posyandu** system (which encompasses community activities to promote maternal and child health) has been a vital piece to combat maternal and child mortality in the country. Within this system, community health volunteers provide reproductive health and antenatal care, and offer information and basic health services. Many women volunteer for this role to monitor the well-being of their own children. However, **Posyandu** activities rely on ad hoc donations from the community and occasionally from public sources, which also means unreliable infrastructure, supplies, and human resources. In deprived environments such as rural Simeulue, the **Posyandu** system struggles to keep its basic operations.

Therefore, babies born into this setting are at risk of severe undernutrition. Although these infants are desired, cared for, and loved just as they would be elsewhere, the environments in which they grow significantly influence their physical and cognitive development. From the time a baby is still in the womb until toddlers become integral to family dynamics, the accounts that follow offer insights into the various voices that shape the care of a new life. Grandparents, husbands, extended family members, neighbours, community health workers, and officials all contribute their beliefs about what is best for the child. These narratives are based on extensive conversations with a pregnant woman, a first-time mother, two healthcare practitioners, and a father in three different locations in Simeulue. They illustrate how access to resources, trust, validation, and the translation of knowledge regarding child-rearing are influenced by social and physical landscapes. Precarious conditions aside, in places like Simeulue, a young child's developmental trajectory is shaped by the beliefs and practices of community members whose perspectives hold power. Whether or not these perspectives align with Western ideals of suitability, health, or benefit, each voice reflects a genuine interest in ensuring that the new members of their community thrive, allowing their culture and people to endure.

Diah: A pregnant mother

My name is Diah. I am 22, and I'm currently in my third month of pregnancy. My husband and I used to live in Sinabang where he was doing some labouring work, but we returned to my parents' village when we discovered I was pregnant. This is common for first-time pregnant women in our culture, as parents are the ones who possess valuable knowledge and experience to advise first-time mothers. We follow their advice. Like many pregnant women here, I've been relieved of most household chores, except for lighter tasks like sweeping. I am not allowed to ride a motorbike, as it is said it can lead to miscarriage. We cannot go out during sun showers or sunset prayer times because these practices are believed to lead to illness for ourselves and our babies. We believe that the baby will get black or develop blue marks. There is a case in this village.

My first months of pregnancy have been quite relaxed. About ante-natal care, some religious leaders see the **Posyandu** negatively, and we are asked not to go. They say injections they give you to support the mother's health are **haram** (contrary to Islamic dietary laws) and may kill the foetus, so some people are afraid of attending the **Posyandu**.

My mother will be heavily involved once the baby is born, and she will make sure our traditional birth midwife comes along to the **Pustu** (community health centre post) when it's time for the baby to come. My mother will bathe, swaddle, and feed the baby from day one. Babies in this village are fed bananas with mashed rice very early on, especially when they cry too much which means there is not enough breastmilk, and they are hungry. There is an abundance of bananas in this area.

Masnun: First time mother of a young child

I am Masnun and my son Amin is a year old. We live in this house you see, which was built by non-governmental organisations (NGOs) after the tsunami, It's built on wooden stilts, and we have a toilet and bathroom in the backyard, separate from the main house. But most houses here don't have a toilet. We live with my husband's brother who is a fisherman, his wife and child, and my mother. We are seven in the house.

When my baby was born, producing breast milk was a struggle during the initial 10 days. My neighbour who had a child of just over one kindly offered to breastfeed my baby. I agreed, but this resulted in my baby having diarrhoea. When my baby turned a month old, I received conflicting advice. The elderly in our village recommended feeding mashed bananas to help the child grow quickly and develop a sturdy body and bones, while the community midwife suggested that breast milk should be the sole source of nutrition at this time. I was confused and decided to give mashed bananas occasionally, as we were all fed mashed bananas as babies. By the time my child reached three months, my grandfather advised feeding boiled, filtered carrots and potatoes mixed with rice. Now Amin is almost one, and we feed him soft rice with vegetables or fish, depending on what is available and how much money we have.

I still breastfeed my child, especially at night and during the afternoon. The neighbours told me I should stop breastfeeding now, as they believe it could make Amin less intelligent. They said that if I breastfeed my baby beyond the age of two, he will become stupid, and it is not breast milk anymore, but blood. They suggested putting something bitter on the breast to stop the child from breastfeeding, but that would make me sad. But I've heard from others about families who breastfed their children until the age of five, and those children were doing well in school. So, I continue to breastfeed. But if my child is crying too much, I give him snacks, like wafers and packaged potato crackers. These can be bought for very little money, anywhere in the kiosks around here.

My child is often sick towards the end of the month, which some neighbours believe indicates intelligence. When Amin is unwell, I give him syrup medication to reduce his fever, which I get from the local health post – my sister-in-law told me about this, from her experience with her own children. I often get advice from her.

My sister-in-law's advice is better than what I could get from the community nurses at the **Posyandu. Kaders**, cannot offer much assistance or information to us, not because they don't want to but because they don't know. They have limited knowledge; they are just like us, non-expert people.

Tofidah: A community nurse (Kader)

My name is Tofidah, and I have served as a **Posyandu** community nurse in this village for the past two years, working alongside my fellow cadre, Resmi. This role found us more by circumstance than choice: we were asked to join as **kaders** by friends who had volunteered for many years and needed people to take over. As a volunteer nurse, you get a minimal stipend to cover transport costs – it's not enough of an incentive, really. Still, our commitment to maternal and child health keeps us going, even though we face many challenges.

Our **Posyandu** activities primarily revolve around measurements, weighing, and recordings of infants' growth and providing supplementary food for the babies when we think the child is not growing as expected. But this **Posyandu's** setting leaves much to be desired. As you can see, it's housed in an incomplete warehouse that often carries the scent of urine and goat droppings, as goats often rest just outside the door. The absence of a dedicated space for **Posyandu** makes everything difficult. We do not have a proper space to conduct the activities we would like to deliver, and of course parents do not feel inclined to come. Which parent would like to bring their baby to a "health post" where there is an abandoned tractor next to the space where we measure babies, and that smells like animal faeces? Unfortunately, our village's **Posyandu** has limited financial support. We receive only a fraction of the funds compared to other villages, which has hindered our ability to provide adequate supplementary food. This is a struggle because we understand the importance of nourishing children, particularly when there are clear signs of malnutrition in our community. We are concerned about this.

Our day-to-day activities occur from 9 AM to 12 PM, but many parents don't participate because they are busy working in their gardens or rice fields. We've tried to emphasise the importance of immunisation and have even provided paracetamol syrup to alleviate parents' concerns about fever, which sometimes follows vaccinations. Many parents are still reluctant to immunise their children out of fear of the child getting a slight fever. Also, some parents reject vaccinating their children as they believe vaccines are not **halal**, or against Islam's dietary laws. Despite our efforts to educate the community on what we know about modern medicine, there are still those who turn to traditional healers or village shamans. The belief here is that prayers can heal children. Additionally, there's a prevailing misconception that a crying baby is a sign of hunger, leading parents to introduce solids like bananas – just as our parents used to feed us – or formula milk, when all the baby needs to thrive is breast milk. What could improve the **Posyandu** system in our village? It is a tough situation. Firstly, we need a cleaner and more appropriate space for our activities; otherwise, parents who are already distrustful of the role we play will be even less inclined to bring their infants to us. We also need more financial support and incentives to get more **kaders** who want to do this job. Most of us are in our 50s. We need younger volunteers. And we need more training, as parents come with questions we have no answers for.

Nur: A health promotion officer

My name is Nur, and I am the head of health promotion in this district. I started as a midwife assisting an NGO's post-tsunami activities in Simeulue, so for the last two decades I have been trying to improve child development and maternal health in our communities. Parenting in Simeulue differs significantly from urban areas like Banda Aceh. In rural settings like this one, it is difficult for the right information to get to families. Although there have been improvements over the years, the situation remains difficult. We still see a lot of undernutrition and disease in young children.

The health promotion unit I manage focuses on disseminating the Ministry of Health programmes, which include monitoring child development through the **Posyandu** system and the **kaders** who volunteer, and we are trying to integrate early childhood education into **Posyandu** activities. We are also working on non-smoking initiatives, as pregnant mothers and young children are very exposed to smoking in this district of Simeulue.

But limited budgets affect the proper implementation of these programmes, and we face challenges in the supervision, monitoring, and execution of these activities.

My major concern is the lack of training for community health volunteers, as it affects their confidence and ability to do their work and gain trust from parents. We have tried to re-establish a more systematic way of selecting **kaders**, but many villages have not yet ratified this initiative. **Posyandu** attendance remains very low. We need greater community awareness and participation, which is a big challenge because in our region traditional medical practices are more trusted than modern medical ones. Recently, the district has prohibited traditional midwives from operating due to high maternal and child mortality rates, but a big proportion of pregnant women still opt for traditional midwives during childbirth. Sometimes they don't have a choice, as many of our villages don't have a resident midwife, but even when they do, younger midwives may lack the confidence to conduct deliveries and end up working together with traditional midwives. We need to improve the capacity of midwifery education. Midwife coordinators at health centres should ideally supervise village midwives, but this is rarely implemented effectively.

Another pressing issue that affects children's health is access to clean water. In many villages, people must draw water from diverse sources, and the quality of the water is not guaranteed. There is still a lack of sanitation facilities in a big proportion of households, and open defecation is very common, not just in Simeulue but across Aceh. So, these precarious environments, added to restricted diets in young children (basically revolving around rice, fish, and occasional snacks), make it so difficult for us to see improvement in children's well-being and prospects.

Aleng: Father of four

My name is Aleng. I am a farmer. We have four children; the oldest is 14, and the youngest is close to five months old. I start labouring in the field at 8 o'clock, then go home for lunch at 12 and then go back to the field after lunch until 5 p.m. Fathers in this community are mainly farmers and fishermen. Most have limited involvement in childcare, but all fathers here engage in evening *Qur'anic* education for their children (teachings based on Islam's holy book, the *Qur'an*). Islam teaches us children are God's gift. So, one of my main responsibilities is to teach my children to recite the *Qur'an*, which we do almost every evening.

You ask me about our children's diet. In this household we have limited financial capacity to buy food, so the family often eats only rice with vegetables and **sambal** (chili paste). But my wife used to be a **Posyandu kader**, not anymore, as she is too busy. So, she knows about children's growth. The youngest is still being breastfed, but when his mother is not home, I give him a bit of water with sugar while we wait for her. I have learned this from experience with my older children. At the age of one, my children started to eat mushy rice and vegetables, sometimes with fish or egg if I had some money. From the age of two, they eat the same as we do. Beef, we eat only once a year for **Ramadan**. I would like to provide better food to the children, but we don't have the capacity at the moment; we don't have enough money. When I have a bit of money, I let them buy snacks such as **roti**

nabati (wafers), especially when they don't want to eat. It is better than not eating at all.

It is my wife who takes the young children to the **Posyandu**. I don't really know what the activities are there. I just sometimes drop off my wife but have never been inside. I know they weigh the children. My knowledge on children's growth comes from my own observation watching others in the community and from my wife. I want my children to become independent. My older daughter helps with the household chores before going to school. On the days they don't have school, children also help planting rice, even my third child, who is in the first year of primary school.

Bridging knowledge and power

In their own ways, Diah, Masnun, Tofidah, Nur, and Aleng help infants survive in contexts where there is a combination of precarious livelihoods, engrained customs around child development, and a poorly resourced maternal and early childhood health system. With no doubt they try their best in caring for and providing for the youngest members in their communities, but tensions and adverse forces interfere in the process.

Dominant beliefs and practices around what is the best nutrition and protection against disease for babies and young children are tightly held in these communities. The accounts above reveal that many of those raising children in Simeulue are convinced about feeding and caring practices that are in misalignment with what health officials would advise. Introducing solid food to babies, such as bananas and rice, very early on has been accepted for generations. Early weaning because breast milk is believed to be insufficient nutrition is also widely endorsed. Mild fevers and babies crying consistently after vaccinations trigger heightened fear in parents and grandparents, often deterring them from trusting immunisation.

Although modern medical appraisals may dismiss and rectify these approaches to infant rearing, the stories above also indicate that behaviours stem from trusted knowledge systems that provide comfort and security to the caregivers. Within these belief systems, the authority that grandparents and religious leaders hold carries significant weight, and therefore medically validated knowledge competes with knowledge that has been held for generations and is still community-endorsed. Fathers also have limited access to alternative knowledge on child development, as in a patriarchal system where caregiving duties are mostly left to women, they have minimal participation in maternal health clinics, at most offering their wives a lift. Religion also plays a role by reinforcing Islamic teachings on what can and cannot be ingested, including considerations for vaccine components. Religious leaders may mandate not immunising children if vaccinations are not approved by Islam. Finally, the people of Simeulue cannot escape the global processed food markets, where cheap and widely available unhealthy snacks serve as an easy solution to crying babies, exposing the "commercial determinants of health" (see Gonzalez, 2019).

Amid this complex cultural setting, unpaid and poorly trained community health volunteers, with a genuine interest in improving the health outcomes of the children in their communities, persevere in their mission to improve the prospects of new lives. Despite all the hurdles and distrust they encounter, **kaders**, through the **Posyandu** system, continue their work as intermediaries between the basic scientific knowledge on child development they can gather and the community knowledge they understand so well. They even incorporate this knowledge into their own child-rearing practices and communications with parents (see Randell *et al.*, 2024).

In rural Simeulue, income is scarce and unstable, and basic infrastructure is precarious. Local communities have developed and reinforced belief systems that mitigate the daily uncertainties and threats of their environment. These belief systems help the islanders feel supported and secure in the critical task of raising the newest members of their communities. Having been harshly affected not only by scarcity but also by natural forces, with the memory of the tsunamis still fresh in their minds, communal approval is paramount.

Therefore, breaking through the imperative of culture to make space for new knowledge on how to help infants develop optimally is a challenge. This may involve improving and enhancing the reputation of the under-resourced **Posyandu** system, which is exclusively staffed by volunteers. Despite being a remarkable testament to community-driven health initiatives globally, it remains underappreciated. It may also involve advancing the emancipation of mothers, enabling them to confidently question deeply rooted community and religious beliefs about health and nutrition. Additionally, educating fathers so they can be more involved in infant care – including supporting and participating in child and maternal health clinics, which currently have only 30 per cent attendance from mothers with negligible father participation – will be important. However, with the robust community support already in place to help infants through their vulnerable early years, people in Simeulue can rely on significant social capital to open the best possible path for their offspring. At the next stage, when children start primary school, they will need strong bodies and minds to shape a promising future for themselves.

* * * * *

Extension activities

To deepen their understanding, students will engage in several extension activities that encourage them to apply anthropological methods to real-world issues of child health and malnutrition.

Extension Activity 1: In small groups, students will research and compare the traditional food beliefs and child-rearing practices in Aceh with those in another region of a different country facing similar issues of under- or malnutrition. They will explore how traditional knowledge intersects with or contradicts medical advice.

Extension Activity 2: Students will participate in a role-playing exercise where they take on the roles of community nurses, parents, or healthcare policymakers in Aceh. They will work through scenarios where health interventions must be adapted to local beliefs and practices in order to be effective and present their strategies for improving trust in healthcare and promoting better nutritional practices.

Extension Activity 3: As a class, students will conduct a case study on the broader social and political context of infant care in Aceh, analysing the role of government programmes, NGOs, and local community leaders in addressing childhood health and overall development. They will then propose an intervention plan that combines both traditional knowledge and scientifically validated practices, taking into account the local cultural context and the realities of healthcare delivery.

3
Language, courage: Schooling as a migrant in inner Sydney, Australia

Learning objectives

By the end of this chapter, students will be able to critically analyse the complex experiences of migrant children of primary school age as they navigate the challenges of starting school in a foreign country. They will gain an understanding of how language barriers, cultural differences, and shifting expectations from both parents and teachers can shape the children's school experiences. Students will explore the emotional and psychological effects of moving to a new country, learning a new language, and assuming new roles in both the school environment and the home. They will also learn about the pressures migrant children face to succeed academically, often under the weight of high parental expectations, while trying to balance the demands of both their adopted country's identity and their original cultural heritage. Furthermore, students will examine the dynamic between parents, teachers, and peers and how these interactions influence the children's sense of belonging and identity.

* * * * *

Children who are lucky enough to have survived the first years of life, who live in places where public education is available to all, and whose parents can afford sending them to school instead of needing their labour, usually start school between the ages of 5 and 6. During this stage, physically and emotionally healthy children begin to display a level of cognitive, emotional, and social readiness that allows them to engage in more structured, demanding, and content-focused learning processes. At this point in their lives, they become capable of grasping more abstract concepts, effectively interacting with peers and teachers, and better managing their emotions compared to when they were younger. Also, their improved attention span, language skills, and fine motor abilities add to the dispositions they need to confront regimented institutions such as schools.

Australia's diverse cultural landscape has for decades been shaped by successive waves of migrant families. In the 1970s, in alignment with a neoliberal policy context where market-driven growth and the promotion of individual entrepreneurial freedom became to dominate the political economy of Australia as well as of many other Western economies, the Skilled Migration scheme signalled a significant shift in Australian immigration policy, moving away from the "White Australia" stance – which favoured European immigrants – to a relatively more open migration scheme, which reflected Australia's growing need for professionals and other skilled workers to support its economic development. Over the years, the Skilled Migration Scheme has seen several changes and refinements aimed at better matching the skills of immigrants with the needs of the Australian labour market. But it has hailed migrants and migrant families from around the world, a big proportion of them representing the middle class, many often equipped with one or more university degrees and accustomed to a high standard of living in their home countries (Richards, 2008).

Currently, the presence of first- and second-generation children from these migrant families constitutes a substantial portion of the youth demographic. Statistics from the Australian government consistently indicate that about one-third of the Australian population was born overseas. For the school-age population, this means that 10 per cent of children were born in another country (about 450,000), more than one-fifth (about a million) have both parents born overseas, and around 16 per cent (over 700,000) have one parent born overseas (Australian Institute of Health and Welfare, 2024).

Sydney and its metropolitan suburbs represent the largest urban area in the country and attract almost a third of the almost 150,000 skilled migrants that enter Australia every year. Currently, 38 per cent of Sydneysiders were born overseas, with migrants from across Asia being the most numerous, but with newcomers arriving from all corners of the world, including Latin America – the region of origin of some of the storytellers in this chapter. School enrolments in Sydney, therefore, reflect the dynamics and diversity of the city's population, with over a third of students coming from households where languages other than English are spoken (NSW Department of Education, 2021).

While attention has been given to how children in migrant families acquire English as a second language and to their academic performance (including how it compares to their non-migrant peers), the nuanced social and cultural adjustments faced by these children and their families, as well as insights into how school teachers and staff engage with them, remain largely unexplored.

Latin American children caught in stories of hope, aspirations, sadness, and frustrations

In Sydney, primary schools can look very foreign to someone coming from cities in Latin America. Physically, primary schools are easily accessible to anyone, with open gates leading to playgrounds, green spaces, and classrooms. Parents, teachers, children, and other school staff can be seen throughout the day on school grounds. Parents are very welcome, especially as volunteers in classrooms and various other activities, including the school canteen. Teaching staff are usually very accessible, and parents typically chat with them informally upon picking up their children. The school day runs between 9 and 3, with some working parents needing to make use of the "before and after school care" facilities offered, usually on school grounds. For Latin Americans encountering Australian schools for the first time, these environments appear to be relaxed, informal, and friendly – a big contrast compared to the often rigid, formal, and academically demanding educational institutions in their countries. But interestingly, this welcomed friendliness and relaxed nature of schools may conflict with migrant parents' high expectations around a child's self-care, discipline, and academic rigour (Amigó, 2017).

The narratives that follow explore the stage of life when children commence formal education. The stories will disclose youngsters' curtailed freedom when institutionalised through school, an experience that is exacerbated for children being formally educated in a new homeland and in a language they can yet not speak. The stories were collected as part of a broader study aimed at exploring the "double transition" children in migrant families go through when migrating to Sydney, Australia. The "double transition" is the transition to settling into a foreign land and the transition to starting formal education. The accounts are based on in-depth interviews with Latin American parents who had recently migrated to Australia with their families and with a school teacher working with recently arrived Latin American students. These three accounts were selected from within a set of over 30 interviews with parents and school staff, as they encapsulated the most compelling themes around migrant families and schools in the study.

Raising migrant children (through the eyes of a Peruvian mother)

Pilar, a Peruvian woman in her 40s, came to Australia with her two young children, dragged by her husband, who had big dreams of getting a better-paid job as an information technology (IT) professional. Reluctantly, and constrained by the lessened financial and decision-making power that comes with being a mother of young children who has temporarily left the workforce, Pilar had to follow her husband.

> Why did I come if I was happy in my country? We had a very good standard of living in Peru. But you come here and start from scratch. My husband had applied for the skilled visa to see if he could get better job opportunities, and to see if it would work out, right? We hadn't really thought too much about it, but the visa was granted, and in less than two years, we were on our way to Australia mobilised by providing a better future to our children … more opportunities for them, I guess. The skilled visa came through and the conditions were that in five months we had to be in Australia. Five months!! Francisco was six and Amalia was a baby. Straight away we enrolled Francisco in private English lessons.

One of the first challenges Pilar encountered as a migrant mother was schooling her six-year-old child. Faced with a husband who had still not found work and a baby, she needed her son Francisco to attend school, regardless of whether he had adjusted to the country or whether he could speak the language of instruction.

> We arrived mid-August, and Francisco started school at the end of September. He had a few weeks to get used to the new environment but, to be honest, he didn't want to go to school. "Let me start in January, Mum. Let me get used to the place first", he would say. But we were a bit stressed, and we had to try for each one in the family to adjust to the new life. I had Francisco's baby sister, so I didn't work, and my husband still didn't have a

job either. He was finding it difficult to secure a job. We were living off savings. So Francisco had to go to school so that my husband could look for a job.

But the double transition for the boy was not easy. For many migrant children, adjusting to a new school environment while meeting their parents' expectations for high academic achievement and learning a new language requires significant courage. The anxiety and pressure Francisco may have felt during those initial days are evident in his mother's recollection of his start at school in Sydney.

> Francisco was very shy at first, didn't interact with the other children. So some days he would wake up and say, "Today, I'm not going to school," and he didn't go. And thank God he then met an Australian boy in his class, Josh, who became his friend. Josh helped him a lot, taught him to speak English, taught him to interact with the other kids, and that's what helped him get on track.
>
> Doing school in a second language provided an extra layer of difficulty for him. I did not know as a mother whether he was understanding what was being taught, or whether he could follow instructions. Probably not. Those first school years were very difficult for Francisco. Academically he was placed in the low achieving groups. And I kept on asking the teachers, "How can we make my son move from the bottom level to the top one?" "Oh, that's a lot of effort and work; he will need to do a lot of work." So my son was always at the bottom of the class, from year 2 all the way towards year 4. I was aware that we had migrated and that he didn't speak English well, but I found it hard to accept he was achieving so

poorly, as in Peru he used to go to a very good private school and did so well. So I said to him, "If you continue like this, we're going back to Peru, and you'll see what school is like in Peru." So when my husband got a new job he suggested moving Francisco to a private school in Sydney, as until then he had been attending the public school, "Look, Francisco is leaving the public school system, he has to improve his school results". I knew it was going to be very difficult for him because he had already changed schools. At the age of 9, this was going to be the third school.

Francisco's poor adjustment to the school system in Sydney – at least in the eyes of his mother – was for Pilar a good excuse to return to her native Peru. Ironically, this was, again, another disruptive move for the boy.

So, I decided to go back to Peru, to provide some stability to the children, and for them to be around the family. But my husband said "No, I'm not going back to Peru, where am I going to find work there? There is no job security, there is crime… Do you realise that the children will need to move schools again?" So I left on my own with the two children. And I said to him, "I'm not coming back. I'm staying in Peru," in the hope he would follow me later. Francisco didn't go to school during that time in Peru, as they don't take children halfway through the year, or for only a few months. But he didn't want to go either. So after six months on my own in Peru with my two children, my husband said he would not return to Peru, and that I should either come back to Australia or we would separate. So I thought coming back to

Australia was best for the children. So, with my two children and my suitcases, again, I returned to Sydney. And we returned, with all my pain. I brought everything I could from Peru. And Francisco started school again in Sydney. The school children welcomed him well, and he was happy.

Once back in Australia for good, the schoolboy had to make sense of the complex layers that were shaping his identity. He was a migrant school child, a non-native English speaker, born in Peru but struggling to be perceived as an Australian, and at the same time feeling pressured by his mother to honour his Peruvian blood.

Francisco feels the Peruvian identity a bit more than his sister Amalia, but only slightly. We send him to Spanish classes on Saturdays. He doesn't like going. Now I can tell that English is his first language, and Spanish is his second language. He has lost a lot of Spanish. I worry because I always try to keep up his Spanish because that will help him in the future, something that when you are a child, you don't understand. And he doesn't like Peruvian dances. When we ask him to dance as part of our Peruvian end of the year celebrations, Francisco does everything possible to avoid it. And he complains, "Oh, Mum, why always Peru, Peru, Peru?" as if I put too much of the idea of Peru in his head. And he doesn't like it.

Francisco's reluctance to embrace tightly his country of origin was also felt by his younger sister, Amalia. This, in turn, has fuelled Pilar's determination to instil their Peruvian identity in her

children. It has become Pilar's daily mission and a constant struggle for Francisco and Amalia.

> Amalia is even more reluctant to speak Spanish. When
> I talk to her in Spanish, she tells me, "I don't understand
> you." When she wants to tell me about a problem or
> something going on in her life, she can only do it in
> English. And she tells me "Can't you understand me,
> Mum?" And to be honest, many times I don't under-
> stand, and she complains my English is not good
> enough. So what I tell them is: "From our house's front
> door inwards this is Peru, and from the door outwards
> it is Australia. The customs in this house are Peruvian. In
> this house, everything is from Peru. Do you see anything
> in this house that is not from Peru? Well then, you have
> to speak in Spanish. I respect that you like Australia, but
> you two need to respect me too, right?"

Like all children, Francisco and Amalia need to feel they belong
in the environment they live in. Since school is where they spend
most of their time, interact with peers, and make friends, they
want to feel included and to speak English. Children's exagger-
ation of Australian culture and practices often leads to their
heritage being dismissed or set aside. Parents' despair at seeing
children being drifted away from their roots will shape particular
child-parent relationships and cross-cultural identities that will
be embodied during the life course.

> My kids and my household have become more
> Australian than I would like to. When I try to watch a
> movie in Spanish, the children come to me and say,
> "Mum, in English please". My daughter Amalia was born

in Peru, but she loves Australia more than her brother; she feels it as her own country. On Australia Day, she gets more excited than the Australian people. She celebrates enthusiastically, sings the anthem, and waves the flag throughout the house; she even makes her dad put up flags in the car. "Let's buy, fish and chips", she tells me. I reinforce the idea that she is also Peruvian, I show her images of Peru, the dances of the *Guainos* and *Suayas*, from Peru. And she says, "Mum, that is beautiful. I know I was born in Peru, but I don't know much about it mum…". She feels Australian.

Accepting a mixed-up upbringing (through the eyes of a Venezuelan father)

Carlos, with his wife Ana, moved to Sydney as part of the exodus of Venezuelans that have been fleeing the beleaguered country for the last two decades. Equipped with respected university degrees and sound professional experience in international organisations in Venezuela, they arrived in Sydney under the skilled migration scheme with their young son and the hope of providing him with a lifestyle that would not entail daily fear.

> In Venezuela, you live in constant fear. We wanted to go to a place where we could live a normal life, especially as we were parents with a five-year-old and wanted our child to grow up in a safe environment. When I used to drop off our son Manuel at pre-school every day in Venezuela, I prayed, "God protect him." It's constant fear. So, we thought, we can't live like this, we need to provide something better to our son. We applied to come to Australia as professionals and here we are in Sydney.

We arrived with a certain amount of money, knowing it would last for some time without a job. But, of course, you start getting concerned about how difficult it may be to get a job, whether the savings will be enough, for how long they will last, and what will happen when it runs out… Those were our concerns, besides fearing living in another language. Because we had some English, but you don't know if that will be enough to get a good job. Work and language were the two things we feared. Manuel had just turned five. And well, he was worried because, despite his young age, he was very mature. He used to say, "I don't want to go to Australia because I don't speak English." He was aware of this problem. He knew what that meant for him – not being able to communicate, not being understood, and not understanding others.

Having just arrived in Australia, with limited savings and the pressure to start looking for jobs straight away, Carlos convinced his wife they needed to put their five-year-old in school immediately. Two days after landing in Sydney, their son Manuel became a Sydneysider schoolboy. He did not speak English. He did not even have the school uniform. But he did not complain.

I don't often cry. But I cried that first day. I remember his face, as we were travelling to school, he looked petrified, completely petrified with terror. He looked out the window, didn't say a word, his face was pale, fearing being left at a school where he would not understand a word. We had just taught him how to ask to go to the bathroom, how to explain when something hurts… three or four basic things. That first day of school was terrifying for me too, very tough, his face was telling me "Don't leave me here."

Unable to communicate in the school environment, Manuel coped as he could. He tried to grasp what was happening around him but felt isolated and lacked the confidence to try and make friends or join playground games. Manuel could not speak English yet, but he became very sensitive to gestures and body language – he needed to survive in this foreign environment.

> He never, ever said he didn't want to go to school. I would say, "How was your day today? Did you play with other children?" And he would say, "No. Today I didn't play, today I sat on the stairs and watched others play". A few days after starting school the teacher called us because Manuel had given a child a big punch. You know how kids are … his schoolmates were teasing him because he couldn't speak English … and although Manuel didn't understand what they were saying to him, he understood the body language. And since he couldn't defend himself with words, what he did was defend himself physically. The teacher told us she could see his frustration, and that's why he reacted violently. Those first weeks were so tough for everyone in the family.

Manuel therefore became obsessed with learning English, as until he could master it, his school life was going to be miserable indeed, not just in terms of failing academically, but also in terms of not being able to make friends and participate in all the fun he could see happening at his school in Sydney. His father Carlos recounts his surprise when his son mentioned he wanted to spend more time at school.

After two or three weeks at school, I picked him up from after-school care where he was attending twice a week, and as we walked towards the train station he told me he wanted to go to after-school care every day. "Why?" And he said, "Because if I go more, I'll learn the language faster… I go to school from 9 to 3, and then I'm at home speaking Spanish". He realised that at after-school care, he spoke and listened to more English for a longer time, and not from the teacher but from his peers, as it is basically play time after school, when he could listen to and use the vocabulary that was most important to him. Language was his main concern.

And finally, one day, Manuel felt the language used at school had become really familiar. He had crossed the boundary between being an outsider and being an insider, a transition that migrant children often become particularly skilled at.

After a couple of months of attending school something curious happened. One day upon picking him up from school, Manuel told me, "The teacher said something to me today in Spanish." "Oh, really?!" I went and asked his teacher, "Miss, Manuel told me you said something to him in Spanish." She laughed and said, "I don't speak any Spanish … the only thing I know is 'hola'! No … what I think is happening is that he's understanding, and he still doesn't realise that I'm talking to him in English." For him, the teacher was talking in Spanish because he was understanding what she was saying.

And once Manuel mastered the currency of language, many other Sydneysider traits followed. From getting around barefoot to playing typical Australian outdoor games, the boy quickly adopted the habits that made him part of inner Sydney's childhood culture. His courage, determination, and efforts to belong paid off.

> Now, two years in the country, English dominates. Even when he plays with his Venezuelan friends he plays in English, his childhood is in English. In his child's world, he sees himself obviously as an Australian. Culturally, he has Australian habits… he likes to walk without shoes, those kinds of things, he likes messy hair. Every time grandma sees him over Skype, she says, "Kid, but that hair….!!" He likes that messy hair because that's how he sees kids here. The games he plays, the way he plays, and everything… At the end of last year, we had the Australian citizenship ceremony. So, I told him, "Son, today we received the citizenship certificates, and we are all Australians now." And he said, "Yes!!!!!!! I don't have to speak Spanish anymore."

With a hint of nostalgia, his father explained that Manuel's Venezuelan identity was being overshadowed by his Australian one. Although Manuel might later reclaim his culture of origin – as often happens with many young migrants – during this formative stage in childhood, the connection between language, self, and place is crucial for a child's emotional development. As Carlos puts it, "He acknowledges he is from Venezuela; he may appreciate it, but it doesn't represent him completely".

A teacher's perspective: It's (not) all about language

Mrs Williams is a kindergarten teacher with over ten years of experience at a public school in a middle-class neighbourhood of inner Sydney, where about half of the students speak a language other than English at home and who need support learning the language of instruction. An expert in working with children from migrant backgrounds and teaching them the English language, she shared, against what is commonly believed, that it takes more time for children than it does for adults to grasp a host country's language upon migration.

> People overestimate how easily children learn a new language. There is a misconception that children pick up a new language faster than adults. Children are learning two languages at once. Adults already know their first language at a high level and can transfer it to a high level in a new language, whereas children are learning two languages and they're not at a high level yet in either. When migrant children first come, what they pick up is playground language. Some parents feel their children will be fluent in English in twelve months, and that is very unrealistic.

The focus on language and "proper" classroom manners was compelling in Mrs Williams' account when asked how she helps non-English-speaking new arrivals settle into the school and into their classes.

> So, that is where we come in, trying to feed the more formal language and written structures into their writing and so on. I try and be explicit from when they first

arrive; about manners, how to ask for things, so that they know how to be polite, and how to relate to people, and sometimes there's differences, for example about volume of the voice, and how far away you are from each other and all those sorts of cultural things… Expectations about how you sit, how you move, sitting on the floor, putting up your hand to talk, and responding to direct questions. For example, here teachers expect students to look at us directly with your eyes to show that you're listening. Not all cultures do that. So it's a big transition for them … there's so many cultural rules that they haven't been exposed to, and when they first come, I mean it's a new world … there are cultural expectations we have that the kids are just being exposed to, so it must be hard, definitely.

For teachers like Mrs Williams, her work with new arrivals does not just revolve around the children themselves but extends to parents and their concerns about how quickly their children are adjusting through the language but also about parents' anxieties about their children losing fluency in their mother tongue.

Parents naturally worry about their children and hope that they're fitting in, and so, they're worrying about their language. They want them to quickly be fluent, which you know does not happen straight away. I have found there seems to be a pattern, and it's just an impression really, that children, when they've been here for a while, and English is starting to become their first language, they're forgetting their home language… And also, they want to fit in with their peers as well. And I've had parents come to me when they've felt upset that their children are speaking back to them in English, and I think well English is becoming their first language and I think that can be really difficult for parents because they want their children to speak their language as well. But at the same time they want their children to be successful in English, so it's a hard, hard thing for children to meet everyone's expectations. I can understand that for parents to see your child lose the mother tongue would be sad. But these children are going through a tough change, and need to feel they belong somewhere, they need to be a bit more like their peers, and they really want to establish English as their first language.

Language being at the centre of children, parents, and teachers' concerns during the initial period of adjustment to school and country, Mrs Williams highlighted how other important questions about the big disruption migration causes in these children's lives often go unasked. Having worked with migrant students for many years, Mrs Williams alluded to the powerlessness of these children in making decisions about such a big move. She disclosed children's frustration, something their own parents are oblivious to.

It's hard to move to any country that's not your own! And you could get homesick as well, and I think, sometimes also depends on the reason why you came. Were you happy to come? Was it a family decision? Were the kids happy to leave? Were they happy to go on an adventure their parents chose for them? Or was it something that they weren't really happy about? I think that really makes an impact on how children experience this transition, and how they are going to view the experience.

> So often, recently arrived migrant children become frus-
> trated. There is so much going on in their minds… they
> want to share and speak, they want to make friends, but
> they can't. It's really frustrating for them.

Mrs Williams' students are indeed lucky to have her, as she is a teacher who can understand migrant children's needs beyond language and considers the contexts and individual histories that exist behind the physical bodies in her classroom. However, not all teachers are as sensitive to migrant students or as well trained to help them. More old-school, academically focused teachers, who are driven by their own and class performance, may take the inability to communicate in English as a learning problem, and in doing so, perhaps contribute to the stigma and lack of confidence that both Francisco and Manuel in the previous stories may have felt.

> I've had kids that just speak to me in another language
> and they know I can't understand it, but they just need
> to say it, and that's why I just nod and think it's great they
> do. There was this Argentinian child who would come to
> me and just speak to me in Spanish, and although I could
> not understand, I just let him talk, because I thought
> "this kid just has to talk, he needs to talk, just get it out"!
> I am more worried about the children that sit there qui-
> etly and don't say anything, and teachers who are not
> trained to identify the reasons behind that behaviour,
> can't find the criteria for marking and reports, and their
> concern is that these children are slow, or maybe there's
> something wrong, and they tend to classify them as a
> child with learning difficulties. Because as teachers we

are accountable for their progress, and unfortunately we pigeonhole students. A lot of migrant children will sit there quietly for six months, not saying a word.

Multiple belongings. Multiple accountabilities.

Many of the families with young children who come to Sydney under the skilled migration scheme do so with the future success of their young children in mind. Already successful professionals themselves, migrant parents are hopeful that the prosperous and safe environment that Sydney offers will enable promising opportunities for their children. Children may disapprove of such a big uprooting move, but being dependents and with very limited decision-making power, they can only follow their parents and become the receptacles of their dreams, aspirations, and also frustrations. These children's own feelings about such a big move often remain muted. And those silenced emotions are exacerbated in their new school environments, where they cannot understand what is being said or express what they would like to say.

In the meantime, many of these children, as most do, feel pressured to please their parents, new friends, and teachers, and even the relatives left back home. With their incipient English language skills, they try to embark on a transition process through which they are progressively integrated into the new cultural world through school. But they are continually referred to their original cultural system prevailing in their families at home. Hence, parents and teachers talked about their children's developing identities in hybrid terms, considering them to be in between cultures, feeling at home and alienated in their new and old settings (Amigó, 2012). Francisco, for example, felt an outsider during his first phase in Australia but also felt out of place in Peru when his mother decided to return with him temporarily. And Manuel, celebrated enthusiastically becoming an Australian citizen but still acknowledges he is from Venezuela. The concept of "multiple belongings" (Vandenbroeck, Roets and Snoeck, 2009) is particularly illuminating, as it sheds light on the dynamics of identity formation in mobile, globalised societies where individuals can adhere simultaneously to various reference groups, such as national, ethnic, and language groups.

The stories recounted by children, their parents, and teachers suggest migrant children become entangled in a crossroads of expectations soon after they arrive in a new country. Their teachers and parents expect them to do well in school and learn the language as well – and as fast – as possible, while their parents also aim to reinforce their children's native culture and language. Their peers – responding to a particular socialisation system – pressure them to assimilate into the mainstream and to discard strong ethnic identifiers. Despite the multiple expectations and the various challenges that children like Francisco and Manuel face in foreign-language classrooms, on the playground, and at home, they still show remarkable courage and a willingness to embrace the new language and environment as integral to their evolving identities.

The initial school years represent a pivotal developmental stage in a child's life; their routine becomes regimented, their social worlds expand, they are exposed to new knowledge, and their academic learning abilities are tested. Importantly, it is during this stage that their social identity begins to take shape – in great part as a reflection of how others perceive them. For migrant children, this is a particularly challenging transition, as they need to add to it the layers of incorporating a new cultural and spatial reality, mediated by a language they need to learn from scratch. Plus, as we will see in Chapter 4, more will be required of children as they enter the pre-puberty years, when their sense of responsibility further develops, instilled by the environments where they live.

* * * * *

Extension activities

To expand on these learning objectives, students will engage in a series of extension activities that encourage them to apply anthropological concepts to the experiences of migrant children in educational contexts.

Extension Activity 1: Students will conduct a comparative analysis of the school experiences of migrant children in Australia with those in another country (e.g., the United States, South Africa, Argentina, France, and Singapore), focusing on challenges such as language barriers, cultural adaptation, and academic pressures. They will explore how schools in different countries support migrant children and compare policies aimed at integrating children into the educational system.

Extension Activity 2: In pairs, students will create a role-playing activity that simulates the experiences of a migrant child navigating school in Australia. One student will take on the role of a child from a Latin American background, and the other will take on the role of a teacher or parent. They will explore scenarios involving language acquisition, peer relationships, and cultural misunderstandings. Students will also discuss the emotional and social challenges faced by the child and propose strategies for better supporting migrant children in their new school environments.

Extension Activity 3: Students will research and present a case study on the role of community organisations, bilingual education programmes, and language support services in helping migrant children adapt to school life. They will then develop an intervention plan that combines cultural sensitivity with educational best practices to help children overcome academic challenges while fostering a sense of belonging and identity in their new school environment.

4
Poverty. Commitment: Contributing to the household in Lombok, Indonesia

Learning objectives

By the end of this chapter, students will gain a comprehensive understanding of the realities of child labour in materially disadvantaged regions of the world, particularly for children in their pre- and early teens who must contribute to the household's survival. They will explore the intricate balance between children's agency, their aspirations for the future, and their commitment to their families in the face of economic hardship. Students will critically analyse how poverty influences children's awareness of their economic value within the household and how external pressures, such as societal expectations around consumption, as well as around the relevance of formal education. Students will also examine the role of local economies and community networks in shaping children's choices and aspirations, as well as how assuming important responsibilities at an early age shapes their personhood.

* * * * *

In most places around the world, children between the ages of 10 and 15 years start assuming a number of responsibilities, which, dependent on the context, can include, besides school, paid and unpaid work, religious, familial, and social commitments. This is also a period of critical physical, emotional, and cognitive changes. In contexts of ingrained poverty, youngsters are key pieces in the survival of their households, and scarcity therefore shapes how young lives evolve at such a critical developmental stage. For better or worse, children growing up in a place where chasing money is a daily ordeal, their understanding of and interactions with the world reflect a sensitivity to their own economic role.

Lombok is a small Southern island in the Indonesian archipelago, with a population of around 3.7 million, and neighbouring famous Bali. Lombok's most important geographical feature is a very fertile central plain about ten kilometres wide that runs from east to west, where most of the population lives. About half of Lombok's population is still rural. The northern half of the island is dominated by Lombok's highest peak, Mount Rinjani, and its auxiliary mountains, while the south is an arid and mostly barren region. The island was successively colonised by the Balinese (eighteenth and nineteenth centuries), followed by the Dutch (first half of the twentieth century) and briefly by the Japanese

(1943–1945). The Dutch took control of agricultural production, attracting vast numbers of peasants to the fertile central plains, who were ultimately trapped in an exploitative economy. Although agricultural production increased markedly due to the new agricultural varieties and technology introduced after independence in 1945, paid work opportunities for the landless were restricted, thus further undermining the living conditions of the majority of the population. Since the end of the colonial era, about a third of Lombok's population has been impoverished and landless (Cederroth and Gerdin, 1986). The Sasak are the indigenous inhabitants of Lombok, making up almost 90 per cent of the island's population. To be Sasak is, by definition, to be a Muslim, and Sasak is their indigenous language – only those who were lucky enough to have access to education also speak the national language, Indonesian.

The eastern regency of the island is marked by a rural-urban divide that is evident in social and political life. Those in urban settings are more familiar with the Indonesian language, "western" clothing, and other aspects of life in a modernising state. But most Sasak live in villages, often in small settlements scattered in the fields. The few hundred residents in each of these small settlements, called **dasan**, naturally comprise the highest concentration of poor, illiterate, "traditional" Sasak. This part of the island is characterised by small landholdings, which are insufficient to provide full-time agricultural work for all household members, so survival relies on a combination of self-subsistence agriculture, paid labour, rental of land parcels, and engagement with middlemen for the production of a variety of crops: rice, corn, cassava, sweet potatoes, coconut, coffee, tobacco, cotton, and sugar. One of these settlements is Dasan Paok, located on the fertile central plain of East Lombok. This hamlet makes a very picturesque scene: the shady, narrow road, lined with coconut trees, meanders through it, framing the majestic peak of Mount Rinjani at its end. Living conditions here are still precarious, with electricity supply being unreliable, no running water, and open defecation still widely practised. This rural, poor, but welcoming environment is the home of truly incredible children, or **kodeq-kodeq** in the local language.

In Sasak culture, children are strongly desired, as without having children, Sasak cannot really be considered adults. **Kodeq-kodeq** are seen and heard everywhere in Dasan Paok, laughing, playing, going to and from school, attending *Qur'an* reciting sessions, carrying or minding infants, sorting tobacco leaves, harvesting rice, doing the dishes in the nearby stream, working in construction sites, hanging clothes on the line, cooking, or minding a tobacco kiln. They are indisputably the soul of the place and the target of an intensive and communal process of socialisation. From around the age of 10, **kodeq-kodeq** get caught up in a dense web of expected demeanours and responsibilities that will teach them how to behave properly, assimilate the Islamic doctrine, and contribute to the household economy. During this period, youngsters have very little power to negotiate and must abide by the conventions set out for them. In particular, they must be extremely respectful of their elders and of adults in general (Amigó, 2010).

There is no sharp division or particular term that marks the beginning of this stage in a Sasak child's life, and its onset depends on the family, and particularly on the sibling composition of a household. For example, an only daughter in a poor household will be pushed to start helping with everyday chores much earlier than a girl from a wealthier household, or where older sisters are already helping. Similarly, children from poorer households will also be urged to start working for money earlier than their wealthier peers. But just as Sasak babies and toddlers are entitled to be pampered during that early span of their lives, during this stage, children have to assume important responsibilities – whether they are poor or not so poor, girls or boys, with older siblings or without them. With almost no exceptions, youngsters are expected to contribute to the everyday maintenance of the household. Be it doing the dishes, looking for firewood, taking rice to the warehouse where it is husked, or minding baby siblings, children of this age spend considerable time carrying out tasks for their households. In a vast number of cases, their contribution also involves bringing cash home, either as a way of helping to cover the everyday expenses of their families or as a way of contributing with the costs they themselves represent (usually school-related) (Amigó *et al.*, 2022).

Another crucial responsibility they must embrace is religion. As up-and-coming members of a strong Islamic community, children must learn how to become good Muslims, and a way in which they achieve this is by regularly attending the informal meetings where a respected and knowledgeable member will teach children (and anyone else) how to read and recite the verses of the *Qur'an*; they refer to this as **mengaji**. They are usually held in private houses or in the **musholla** late in the evening, and their frequency varies depending on the time of the year, but they can even take place daily in a quiet working season. Finally, there is also strong social pressure for children to complete primary school. This is a legacy of the New Order regime of Suharto's 32-year regime (1967–1998), which, despite its widespread corruption and authoritarian control of the country's political life, succeeded in ensuring the schooling system penetrated into every corner of the archipelago and in making basic education accessible and compulsory (OECD/ADB, 2015).

During the rainy season, when many children worked in the nearby river gathering sand to be sold for construction, I used to sit there on the riverbank and watch the scene. It was a good time for chatting with those who were taking a break from the water or who were just looking around or playing. They would come and sit by my side, drawn by their ongoing curiosity about my presence as an outsider in their village. As the rainy season started six months after I had arrived in this locality to conduct ethnographic fieldwork on child workers, these children were used to my presence and happy to confide in me their stories or answer a few of my questions. These happened in friendly conversations, often adorned with laughter and humour, and seldom with hints of sadness or complaints. I thoroughly enjoyed talking to these children, who would also ask me myriad questions. After these brief encounters, I would come back to where I was staying to note down my observations and conversations with my young friends. The stories below were recreated based on more extended field notes of those informal conversations with four of these children.

Children's work

Irwan (male, 11)

I am 11. My dad passed away in Malaysia when I was 5. He had gone as a migrant worker to earn money with the hope of providing a better standard of living for our family but never came back. And no one really knows what happened. And so, I grew up with my mother and two older sisters. Every day is a bit of a challenge: the loud morning mosque prayers wake me up at dawn. I don't have much time to waste. I quickly run to the stream, which is about 50 m away, splash my face, and wash my feet with the little water that runs in the dry season. I go back home to do my prayers, and soon after that, my mother asks me to get whatever water I can get from the well at the back of the house. School starts at 7, and I put on my school uniform (a dark red pair of shorts and a white shirt), which feels very tight as I am growing quickly. It is also often dirty, as I only have one set, and neither my mother nor my sisters can wash it daily. They are very busy working for other people planting rice. In any case, many of the stains would not come off. My family needs money, as all that was gained during the tobacco season has been spent. I miss the tobacco season, when there is a lot of work then for children like myself, placing tobacco leaves on poles to be dried or guarding the tobacco kilns through the night to ensure the temperature is right and the leaves won't be burnt out. Even if I cannot sleep during those nights, it's exciting for me to know that I am responsible for that process and that at the end of the season I will get cash. **Cari uang** or chasing money is an every-day ordeal here, and when the tobacco season is over, the jobs available are not that much fun and are very poorly paid. I don't have a choice really, as my mother and sisters need whatever money I can bring home.

I love school, and especially math. I take after my mother, who never went to school but makes daily mental notes of every bit of income and expense, and without ever having used a note-book and pen, she keeps track of all household finances, including savings and **utang** or debts. Everyone here has some kind of debt. The teacher has told me that I am **pintar** (smart) and that I should really convince my mother to let me attend secondary school. What I would really like is to become a police officer. I am lucky to be a boy; boys have much better chances of being allowed to complete secondary school than girls do. It is expensive to buy school uniforms, but also it's a lot of time allocated to an unproductive activity, let alone the two hours I would have to spend daily walking to and back from school. Neither of my sisters completed secondary school, but I know my sister Rodah, who is now 16, would have loved to. My eldest sister is 19 and about to get married. The wedding will be expensive, and the family needs to save.

Sam (male, 12)

My household is one of the poorer ones, and it is worse for two reasons: (1) we don't have land, and (2) I don't have sisters. My mother always says she would have loved to have daughters to alleviate her work. We are just three brothers; I am the middle one and am 12. Myself and my older brother of 14 have to do many of the chores girls would do, like the dishes and hanging clothes, so that my mother and father can go out and **cari uang** (chase money). Our younger brother is still little. Before and after school I do chores, and when there is an opportunity for money, I also have to go and get it; otherwise my parents get really angry. Even my mother has to gather sand from the river together with me and my older brother. This is a child's job, but we don't have many other options during the rainy season. If my mother sees I am playing too much with the other children, splashing and swimming instead of getting sand, she chases me and hits me with a stick. But I understand, because do you know how much I eat? I usually eat at least two plates of rice for breakfast, lunch, and dinner, so of course I have to work. We are poor, and I am an expense.

During the tobacco season, I tie up tobacco leaves before they go into the kiln. That is much better than getting sand from the river. Many children can keep the money they earn for this job, but I can't. I have to hand it all to my parents, who try to save by buying kids. Once they become young goats, we sell them. My mother became so attached to one of the goats that she didn't want to sell it. But at the end of Ramadan last year, we had no money at all, and we had to sell this goat. It was slaughtered in front of our house by the neighbours who had bought it for a Ramadan feast. My mother was so upset and couldn't stop crying. But that is how it is: money comes in, money goes out.

Rehan (female, 14)

I am 14 and live with my aunt and uncle. My mother died when I was about 5, so my aunt, who is my mother's sister, looked after me when I was a young girl. I am older now, so I look after myself and feel I am independent. I completed primary school and never even considered anything else in relation to school. Who would support me to do that? I never met my father, and I have no siblings. But I do have young cousins, whom I look after almost daily to allow my aunt to earn money. I ensure they are fed, entertained, and clean. I carry the little one, who is not even one, around the village in my **selendang** (shoulder cloth). That gives me free hands to do some household chores. My other two little cousins are two and three and are more independent, so they roam around the village and do not require so much work. But the baby is getting heavy, and that has started to give me back pain from carrying him around all day. I know that soon he will be walking, so that's OK. Mothers here carry their babies all the time, every day, so I shouldn't complain. Some older boys without sisters have to do it too with young siblings, but they are teased. You would never, however, see a man carrying a baby in a **selendang**. Women do all the work. You get up, and after praying, you go and get water, help prepare breakfast, and help feed the children, go to the stream to do the dishes, come back to get the dirty clothes, and go back to the stream to wash them. Then hang them up, and it's time to prepare lunch, which is difficult when there is no money, especially in the rainy season. When my aunt comes back from working on the plantations around midday, I can then go to earn a bit of money myself, either harvesting rice or doing a bit of sand mining, which I hate. I am getting too old for sand mining anyway. Maidens like myself shouldn't do it, as being in the water reveals your body shape, and men look at you; it's embarrassing, and I feel vulnerable. But what do you do when there is no other way to earn money? The tobacco season is good because I can earn my own money and at the end of the season buy something for myself, like a top or even some gold jewellery. If I am able to afford even the smallest gold jewellery, that is good because it's a saving. Or I can also pawn it if I need money. Most women do that in the rainy season when there is no paid work and they need money to feed the family.

Women whose husbands are in Malaysia do this a lot because they are left alone for months, sometimes years, without the husband's income. You ask me what my dream in life is. To become a mother.

Marriuni (female, around 13)

The rainy season is tough. As there is no more work in the tobacco fields for the next six months when tobacco is planted again, all I can do to **cari uang** (chase money) is to collect sand from the riverbed. Sand mining is such a tough job. You get into the river with a bucket and get as much sand as possible and start piling it up on the side of the river. It is exhausting, and you get skin rashes that really sting and often get sick. Each family has its own pile, and then we sell it to the traders who come in small trucks and resell it on construction sites. They are very cheap, those traders; we need to negotiate the price so much. They give us almost nothing for a truckload of sand. It takes at least five days to gather sand for a truck's load. During the rainy season on school days I work about four hours, and on Sundays I work all day. My mother works with me. This is a child's job, but we are so poor that my mother has to earn money in whatever way is possible. We don't have any land to grow our own food. We are seven siblings, and my father left when I was little. I don't even remember him. I feel so sorry for my mother; she often has nervous breakdowns.

I don't know how old I am, as my mother is illiterate and didn't take note of when I was born. But no one really cares about a special birth date as I know they do in other parts of the world. But I am in grade 5 of primary school. I am really bad at school;

I don't understand what the teacher talks about, and I struggle to complete any task. School makes me feel stupid. I wish I didn't have to go and that I could help my mother more. I don't even have shoes to go to school, so I have to go barefoot, and that makes me feel embarrassed. What is the point of school? I learn more working and talking to people. It is a waste of time when I could be helping my mother earn more money so that she doesn't struggle so much to try and feed us. My mum hopes that my sisters and I will get married early so that she has less of a load in trying to feed us all every day. So I think this may be my last year of school. I can't wait to quit school. I know my mother wants the best for us. All I want is to make her life easier.

Critical extra hands

From the beginning of my fieldwork, I was amazed that young children had such a strong sense of responsibility and a clear understanding of the value of their contributions to their households. Not surprisingly, children from very poor households are starkly aware that their work is crucial, be it paid, unpaid, or household work. For female-headed households, as are the ones in Irwan and Marriuni's stories above, their commitment to the survival of the family was particularly impressive. But even children from better-off families are also very mindful of the importance of helping in the household or of earning their own money, even when their parents do not explicitly require it. Commitment is probably the most appropriate word to describe this attitude of children from rural East Lombok. Children are socialised to appreciate the strains of making a living: the unsteady availability of work, the low pay, and the difficulty of meeting everyday needs. It is not surprising that children place an enormous value on money, because they know how harsh it is to make it. They are also aware that helping in the household with everyday maintenance tasks such as cleaning, cooking, bringing water or firewood, and even minding siblings means that their parents or carers are relieved from these chores and thus will have more time for paid work.

Children are also very conscious of the expense they represent for their family. Food, schooling, and clothing signify heavy costs for the household's economy, and, without children's economic assistance, the strain to meet these would be intolerable. In many cases, children intend that their economic contribution to the household will palliate the costs they generate. Likewise, they show support when someone in their extended family needs help, such as an auntie needing help with child-minding or an uncle and aunt building a house. These children learn about their responsibilities and why they should be serious about them. Children of this age learn to take life as a challenging experience. Life is tough, and children in this context cleverly unfold their sense of duty to the survival of their households and communities in any way they can. For the poorest of households, marrying off children sooner rather than later will reduce the number of mouths that need a feed.

* * * * *

Extension activities

To deepen their understanding of these issues, students will engage in several extension activities that will help them apply theoretical knowledge to real-world situations.

Extension Activity 1: Students will conduct a comparative analysis of child labour in Lombok with that of another region or country facing similar economic challenges, such as rural areas in South Asia or Sub-Saharan Africa. They will focus on comparing the types of work children are engaged in, the socio-economic conditions that drive child labour, and the cultural attitudes towards education and family responsibility. Students will then present their findings and discuss potential strategies for addressing child labour without undermining children's agency or family dynamics.

Extension Activity 2: Students will engage in a photo essay project (using Creative Commons-licensed images) that captures the daily life of a child worker in a selected region of the world. The photo essay will focus on children's work, family life, aspirations, and the social pressures they face. Each student will write a reflection accompanying their images, which will highlight the complexities of child labour, the balance between family commitment and individual aspirations, and the broader economic and social factors at play.

Extension Activity 3: In small groups, students will create an economic model that demonstrates the household financial pressures experienced by families in Lombok, considering factors like income generation, cost of living, and educational access. They will then propose a policy intervention designed to reduce the need for child labour while ensuring that children's economic contributions and aspirations are acknowledged and respected. Students will present their proposed intervention, discussing the challenges and ethical considerations of implementing such a policy in the context of Lombok's economy.

5

Marriage. Grit: Marrying young in Sunsari, Nepal

Learning objectives

By the end of this chapter, students will have a nuanced understanding of the social, cultural, and economic factors that contribute to early marriage, particularly for adolescents in their mid- to late teens. They will explore how marriage is often perceived as a naturalised and inevitable part of life, deeply embedded in economic imperatives, family alliances, and gendered expectations. Students will examine the intersection between traditional customs around marriage and the influence of new technologies, including social media, which have introduced new patterns of courtship and relationships. They will critically assess how early marriage conditions young people's life opportunities, may contribute to gender inequality, and place significant burdens on young women in terms of household labour and caregiving responsibilities. Students will also explore the psychological and social consequences of early marriage, including the challenges of navigating sexual and reproductive rights.

* * * * *

Everywhere and anywhere, there comes a time when older children separate from the family unit to form their own household units. The institution of marriage is a cultural form of the human species that has enabled this process of separation by also efficiently enabling the production and care of offspring, the protection of wealth, and the reinforcement and preservation of social groups based on class, caste, ethnicity, or religion. As with most cultural formations, marriage takes diverse forms across geographical regions and historical times but also entails many similarities. For example, across very diverse settings, there are fascinating structural similarities around the practices of dowry or bride-wealth, the patterns guiding where the new household unit will be based, or the adoption of spouses' new personal names after marriage or the bearing of children. Although in contemporary societies some of the rigid social norms governing marriage have loosened, we can still find traces of those norms in current-day practices, including gift-giving in weddings, property transfer from parents to newlyweds, choice of where the new couple will live, and extended family support for raising new family members.

Marriage is, therefore, a deeply socially conditioned practice, and so is the decision of when is the right time to become a husband or a wife. We know that in contemporary Global North settings, the age at first marriage has been delayed considerably, especially since the second half of the last century. There are a range of reasons for this, including women's empowerment, their increased participation in the labour market, access to contraception, and improved and extended access to education. However, in the "majority world", in contexts of economic adversity, balancing the economic cost of providing a house and a home for an adolescent child against the potential benefits of securing their future through conjugal unions has been an ongoing consideration for parents. As suggested at the end of Chapter 4, for families entrenched in poverty, the pressure to have their children marry at a young age can partly stem from the stark reality that pursuing further education is not feasible – usually due to parents finding it irrelevant to their children's likely futures or due to formal education being geographically or financially inaccessible. But alongside this economic rationale, early marriage is likewise a practice entangled in deep social norms, which individuals feel compelled to follow to fit in within their communities. Clearly, parents who promote the early marriage of their adolescent children do it as it is seen as socially acceptable, sometimes even expected by their community. And young people who make the decision to get married at such a young age may likewise face widespread support. And therefore, "child marriage", or the marriage of individuals under 18 as defined by the 1990 United Nations Convention on the Rights of the Child, is a common reality in most of the Global South or "majority world". Although the practice can be more conditioning to girls' rather than boys' futures, in many societies young people of both genders are subject to the societal pressures of marrying young.

In South Asia, about 30 per cent of children get married before they turn 18 (UNICEF, 2022). Nepal has the third highest incidence of child marriage in this region and is the only country in South Asia with a significant prevalence of child marriages among both boys and girls. In 2019, one in five Nepalese women and one in ten Nepalese men between the ages of 20 and 24 were married before their 18th birthday (UNICEF, 2019), and in some remote areas the percentage of girls getting married under 15 can reach up to 83 per cent (Jensen and Thornton, 2003). Early marriage in Nepal has been associated with families' low socioeconomic and educational status, rural or remote geographical location (the practice is much more prevalent in rural areas), financial situation, caste, ethnic group, and religion, compliance to the dowry system[2] (entailing transfer of wealth from the bride to the groom's family), as well as endorsed by communities' views on family honour. Girls are particularly affected by these last two: the dowry system and keeping the family honour. In most regions, as a girl gets older, the dowry becomes more expensive, the pool of potential grooms more limited, and keeping the family honour intact more challenging – a daughter seen flirting or having physical contact, let alone getting pregnant outside marriage, may be considered a disgrace to her family (Hofer, 2020; Guragain *et al.*, 2017).

Early marriage in the Terai (lowlands)

Terai is the term used to refer to the lowland region in southern Nepal and northern India. In Nepal, the **Terai** lies south of the outer foothills of the Himalayas and comprises about a quarter of Nepal's territory. Geographically, the area is characterised by tall grasslands, scrub savannah, forests, and swamps. It hosts 20 of Nepal's 75 districts and close to half of Nepal's population of around 30 million. The region is agriculturally rich and is dominated by plantations of rice, wheat, sugarcane, forest-based industries, and livestock farming. The economy entails a significant proportion of subsistence agriculture, as well as trade with neighbouring India. The **Terai's** population is predominantly Hindu and very ethnically diverse, with more than 120 different ethnic groups. Low-caste, landless farm workers form a significant part of the population and have remained economically disadvantaged for generations. Also, for centuries, the **Terai** has been an arena of population movement, today experiencing massive flows of people crossing daily between Nepal and India, enabled by open border policies.

Sunsari District is in the eastern part of Nepal's Outer **Terai**. It extends over 1,257 km² and is known for its fertile agricultural land, which supports a significant portion of Nepal's rice production. Unemployment among young, uneducated youth is widespread. Major towns include Itahari, Dharan, Biratnagar, and Inaruwa. The district is prone to environmental degradation triggered by deforestation, soil erosion, and water pollution from industrial and agricultural activities. Natural disasters, particularly floods during the monsoon season, add an extra layer of hardship to this portion of the **Terai**.

Seasonal migration to India to earn wages and send remittances back home has been a common practice to escape poverty, but for some of the poorer families, these temporary relocations to India also mean the reduction of their land parcels, as land is sometimes sold as a way of financing trips to the neighbouring country, but also marriage, dowries, and lavish parties as part of wedding ceremonies or death rituals (Sunam, 2015). In this context, deeply ingrained traditional practices like early marriage coexist with technologies such as mobile phones. Such technologies have expanded possibilities, networks, and cultural practices, and marriage is no exception. The stories that follow belong to young married people in Sunsari. They reflect the links between poverty, marriage, tradition, the impact of social media, young love, and the human need to bear offspring. Above all, they tell about how the transition between childhood and adulthood operates in this part of the world, where Global North discourses on women's liberation or youth empowerment and progression through education are oblivious to the rigid environments that keep young people confined to their economic and cultural reality.

The stories were collected within the context of an international NGO programme aimed at reducing the incidence of early marriage in Nepal. The NGO, called Restless Development Nepal, implemented a three-year, multi-pronged educational approach in Sunsari and other regions of Nepal, aimed at generating awareness of the consequences of early marriage amongst adolescents, teachers, and parents. As part of this programme, called "Save the Date", quantitative and qualitative data was gathered from close to 900 individuals, including young people (many of them recruited through high schools selected by the NGO). This programme was an ambitious undertaking that lasted three years, covered three geographical regions in the country, and targeted a range of people (besides young individuals and students, parents and teachers, government officials, health workers, and community-based organisations were included) (Amigó and Gurung, 2021). Such an aspirational intervention needs to be understood in the context of several interlinked social movements and public health campaigns during the last five decades.

Among these are the United Nations Declaration of the Rights of the Child, ratified by 196 countries in 1990; the ongoing upsurge of feminist movements; the promotion of access to universal education as a human right; and the increasing evidence about the risks associated with bearing children at a young age. More recently, the goal to achieve gender equality and girls' and women's empowerment was endorsed by all United Nations member countries in 2015 as part of the 2030 Agenda for Sustainable Development, exerting extra pressure on governments to address early marriage. In 2016, the Government of Nepal endorsed a national strategy to end child marriage by raising the legal age for marriage to 20, empowering girls, mobilising families and communities, and strengthening related services, laws, and policies (MWCSW, 2016).

The stories recreated below, based on interviews with young people who got married under the age of 18, speak of the huge gap that may exist between legislation and practice, of the complexities surrounding child marriage in specific contexts, of the difficulty to govern the private life of individuals and communities, and of the unrealistic expectation that decisions around marriage can be isolated from the economic realities of the materially disadvantaged.

Sarita, smitten and married at 16: Driven by family honour

Sarita is 18, got married just as she turned 16, and lives in a semi-rural area about 30 minutes away from Dahran, a major town in Sunsari. She lives with her two-year-old child, parents, a married older brother, and a younger sister, plus some extended family (her uncle and wife). She belongs to the Rai caste, a group of people with a rich cultural heritage, including elaborate practices around marriage and death. The Rai reside primarily in the eastern parts of Nepal and have traditionally been farmers, living in nuclear families that usually entail two generations. Their belief system has been based on animistic nature and ancestor worship, which is today syncretised into the major religions most of the Rai identify with. Interestingly, 5 per cent of the Rai are Christians – a large proportion indeed for the one ethnic group, as less than 10 per cent of Nepal's population is Christian (Rai, 2018). Sarita is one of them, and her days start with morning prayers, followed by household work.

> Every morning, our family rises at 4 in the morning. We gather in a room for our morning prayers. We are Christian, like many others in our village, and after our prayers, we start our day. While my baby, Nani, is still sleeping, I prepare food to sell in our shop and make tea for the entire family. My sister-in-law also lives with us and helps me with the baby when she can. Later, I handle the chores—cooking dinner, cleaning, and doing the dishes

Sarita's family owns a humble street shop that sells meat cuts and take-away meat treats. Together with other family members, she is responsible for preparing the meat rolls that sell every day in the family's stall.

> I begin cooking the meat rolls around 6 in the morning and by 3 in the afternoon all the meat rolls will be ready. Customers start arriving at the shop around 4 p.m. to purchase the rolls. We also cut meat and sell it to them.

In the evening, our family gathers to eat together around
6 p.m. After dinner, we wash the dishes and discuss our
day's work.

Sarita married outside her own caste when she was 16, based on
her own choice of partner. "Love marriages" are indeed becoming
more common in Nepal. With the widespread access to mobile
phones and social media, even in the poorest of communities,
meeting potential romantic partners online has expanded the
ways young people socialise (Regmi *et al.*, 2022). Getting exposure to a broader range of romantic partners compared to the
ones parents could choose for their daughters has given young
Nepalese women a bit of autonomy around choosing a partner
compared to previous generations. Sarita recounts that her parents were supportive of her "love marriage", even though her
husband belongs to a different caste and a different religion.
Christians in rural Nepal may be more open to inter-caste marriage and marriage that is not arranged by parents (Kirchheiner,
2016). The pressure to keep the family honour, added to the fact
that parents are not able to control their children's exposure to
romantic relationships enabled by social media, may mean families like Sarita's strongly support the early marriages of their children. Sarita's family's reputation in the community is important;
they need to keep on having customers who buy their products;
otherwise, how would they survive?

In the past most people did not support "love marriages,"
they preferred arranged marriages. So, I am deeply grate-
ful to my family for supporting my marriage, even when
Sandeep, my husband, is not a Rai but a Karki. We basically met over Facebook. He is a couple of years older,

and when he moved to my school when I was in Year 10, he sent me a Facebook request, which I accepted and we started being friends on Facebook, and then seeing each other after school. It was a secret relationship and I didn't like that. Even my friends didn't know about it. Sandeep was a Karki and a Hindu, and I was afraid my family would not support this. At 16 I got pregnant, and no one knew. I was scared, I was very scared, but Sandeep told me he would support me in every situation. He proposed to me and then I told my family I wanted to marry him. I had to disclose I was pregnant, and my family had to support my marriage. I did know the law says not to marry until you turn 20, but what was I going to do? Ruin my parents' life and business? We couldn't register the marriage or the birth of the child, but we did get married.

It is common practice for newlyweds in this region of Nepal to go and live with the groom's family. The practice of dowry in some way is connected to the fact that a married daughter's in-laws will be responsible for homing her, which, even if this is not permanent, will incur an expense for the groom's family. In reality, however, a newlywed young woman moving into her husband's family home in this region ends up becoming responsible for a whole range of household chores, in the same way Sarita's sister-in-law is in charge of several chores in Sarita's parents' household. However, being a Christian and a Rai, Sarita felt very unwelcome when she moved into Sandeep's household, which is Hindu and belongs to the Karki caste. Sandeep's family is even poorer than her own. His father had passed away, and his mother and sibling rely on a small parcel of land where they grow rice and some vegetables, which they can occasionally sell.

> When I moved in, I had to do all the chores plus look after my small baby. It was exhausting, as Sandeep was away from the house most of the day working in the land. He did not have a paid job. Couldn't buy much. So, he has now gone to India to get some paid work, and I said to him I could not stay with his mother as I had no help.

Sarita then moved back in with her parents, where her life is slightly easier, as she can share some of the household chores and get some help with child-minding. Sarita expects Sandeep to return for the Hindu festivities, and if he can bring enough money, they may be able to build a small house. In the mean-time, they communicate via Facebook.

Sarita's domestic situation has improved but now faces the diffi-culties in trying to pursue tertiary studies. Post-secondary educa-tion or training is particularly tough for young women in Nepal, mainly because of the high cost of transport and the impact of young women's absence from the household, where they are needed to look after children of their own and help with chores and other family responsibilities.

With the support of her parents, Sarita was able to finish high school and now has intentions of completing a management course at a college in a nearby town, as her parents think this may help with the family small business. However, she is aware this will be challenging. Sarita mentioned the cost of transport to get to the college is about Rp 800 weekly (about US$6), and buses are very unreliable; sometimes they don't even run as the condition of the roads is appalling, especially during the monsoon season. Also, classes run from 11 AM to 3 PM, and although she could ensure she has completed her daily meal preparations for the family's meat stall by 10, her sister-in-law is now pregnant and is not always available to look after Nani.

> I like to read; I really like to read when I find the time. When I was young, I dreamed of being a teacher. I don't think this will be possible as this requires a lot of study, and how can we support that? But I will support my own daughter to study.

Laxmi, eloped and married at 17: Driven by motherhood

> When I was a girl, I had to take care of my family, and now that I'm a woman, now that I am a daughter-in-law, I have to take care of two families. I have to take care of my family, and I have to take care of another family. That's how it is now.

Laxmi is 19 and has been married since she was 17 through "elope marriage," a trend that has become common in Nepal since the 2010s. Elopement occurs when a young couple who is fearful of their respective families accepting a relationship that was made possible due to the unrestrictive ease of communication enabled by social media runs away to make a statement that they want to be together regardless of whether their families approve of the union or not. Young couples usually find refuge in friends' or extended family homes for a few days. Just before the situation becomes a scandal, parents contact their fleeing children, reassuring them that they are welcome to come back, acknowledging them as a couple. Short, informal weddings follow, and the couple is then recognised as a married pair.

> When I was 13, 14, I felt society looked at me in a hostile way. I didn't like that. I felt vulnerable. In year 9, at 14, an older boy at school started sending me Facebook messages and we started chatting with each other and we became very close. He proposed to me. We started discussing elopement. We kept it a secret. At that time, we didn't tell anyone. We eloped and got married a few days later. I had to move to my husband's *maiti* [parental home].

Although social media and non-traditional values seem to have "freed" young people to date and find partners outside their immediate environment, older generations in this area of Nepal talk about social media, and Facebook in particular, as the biggest curse that has come upon them. It has disrupted parents' surveillance of their children and their influence on their children's marriages. In this sense, the younger generations have developed some autonomy around inter-caste communications and friendships and partner choice. For young women like Laxmi, who grew up in a very poor, illiterate family, Facebook expanded her networks and provided a shortcut to achieving a short-term goal she had: to find a partner and become a mother. She now has a one-and-a-half-year-old child.

> I liked to think of the feeling of being a mother. Not many people of my age get the feeling of being a mother, but I did…

Elopement in this area of Nepal does not waive a bride's family's obligation to transfer wealth to the groom's family. In some cases, like in Laxmi's case, the dowry is not monetary but in-kind. A wide range of items are transferred from the bride's family to the groom's. Laxmi described it as a "farewell gift," signalling the parents are sending off their daughter to a new family with goods (this can involve television sets, a mobile phone, furniture, and jewellery), as a love gesture to their child and as a way of reciprocating their daughter's new host family for homing her. In reality, though, for poor families like Laxmi's, this appears as an unfair transfer of wealth, firstly, because the bride's family will remain poorer and secondly, because the amount of work the young wife will provide to her in-laws will greatly surpass the value of the dowry. Laxmi's routine now revolves around a never-ending sequence of housework.

> I wake up at 5, wash my face, go to the washroom, make tea and serve food for all the family. After that, I wash all the utensils and clean the kitchen and the house. My baby wakes up around that time. I feed her and change her and my mother-in-law entertains her. I then light the fire and start cooking again for the family's lunch. When the food is ready, we will eat together as a family. After that, I will wash all the utensils and clean the house again.

Laxmi's husband, Rabin, is also preparing to go to India to do some seasonal work. His family is poor, and there are very limited opportunities for paid work for young men like himself who didn't finish school. Laxmi mentioned her husband does not have a current stable income, just doing agricultural work when he can find it. She may follow him to India in a few months, once he finds a place to live. Laxmi communicated determination to shape a better future for herself and her child. And although Laxmi did not mention this explicitly, her account of daily house-work duties for her husband's family may be yet another reason for her plan to work abroad.

> If I live in Nepal, I want to work in a permanent job and eventually have our own house. But if I don't get a job, I want to work abroad in India. My husband is support-ing me in this.

Laxmi did not mention any regrets about getting married at 17. She mentioned her family supported her, and her husband's family does not mistreat her. However, her daily load of house-hold responsibilities for her "two family units" means time has become a very precious resource.

> I had to lose a lot of my freedom to get married. Now, I have to make time for myself. I have to find time. When the baby sleeps, when I put her to bed in the evening, and before she wakes up in the morning, I have to make time for myself.

Kaajal, vulnerable and married at 17: Forced to marry

> "My husband says that I should give him whatever he wants, out of my own happiness".

At 18, Kaajal has not had a good run in the first stages of her life. Born into a poor, rural, isolated community in Sunsari, her mother died when she was about two. Her father remarried, but he showed no interest in raising his daughter; neither did his new wife. Kaajal was left to live with her maternal grandfather. But he also passed away when she was in primary school. One of her aunts took her under her wings, so Kaajal was able to get close to finishing high school – but she never did. Marriage got in the way.

> Growing up I didn't have a mother at home. I used to think that if I had had a mother, she would have been a good mother, and I would have been a good daughter. Who loves me the most? It is my older aunts who love me the most, but my younger aunts don't. And my in-laws love me a little bit. They do not always appear to accept me.

At 17, Kajaal sent a Facebook request to a boy who was a year younger. They started seeing each other and became close. Kajaal had never felt so cared for, supported, and understood. She fell in love.

> I saw him on Facebook. I sent him a friendship request. I felt he understood all my feelings. He understood everything and he shared everything with me. I would do the same. He supported me when I was in pain. He understood that I had had to bear many bad things in life, and he understood what my father did to me. That's how I came to like him. I felt safe with my boyfriend. I was happy.

As happens in many poor areas of Sunsari, two young people being in love raises community concern. Sights of young people seen having physical contact publicly are unwelcome. Sexual education is still broadly unheard of in traditional communities. Teachers, parents, even health workers mention they feel very uncomfortable raising these topics. So marriage appears as the most practical solution, especially when there is widespread community support, and in situations like Kaajal's, where her fragile household struggles to make ends meet. The opportunity to marry off daughters, especially to wealthier families within the same caste who may provide a more promising future, is laden with societal expectations and pressures. Refusal of such proposals can lead to profound humiliation for the family of the young woman. So even if Kaajal had no intentions of getting married, she really had no choice. Her boyfriend belonged to the same Dalit caste, and his family was promoting the wedding with minimal dowry.

> Of course, I know about the law in Nepal that you can only get married after 20, but my family forced me to get married. My aunts forced me to get married. I know it's not good to get married at such a young age. It's not good at all. But my family would say, "You will do it, it will happen, there will be a wedding." I said, "I won't do it." And they would say, "you will do it".

The few months Kaajal enjoyed while she was getting to know her boyfriend and falling in love are now just one of her happy memories. Life for her has changed again, to a new location, a new host family, a new routine, and even a new facet of her husband.

> Before, I was free to do many things. I could get out of home and do many things. Now I have to ask for

permission to go out. Now, they can say "no". I had to drop out of school because of this marriage. I am burdened with extra responsibilities. My responsibility is to help my mother-in-law and look after her. There is a lot of work at my husband's house. I have a lot of farm work to do. I wake up around 5 in the morning and do the household chores. I cook rice and prepare breakfast. After that, I feed the goats. I feed the chicken, and after that I go to the fields to work, then I go home in the afternoon, and after that I cook dinner and eat with my husband before he goes fishing. Sometimes my husband doesn't support me, and I feel like I'm dying. And if I die, what will happen? My life will be gone. But sometimes I feel like I'm going to be strong and take care of myself.

Kaajal's life is tough indeed, and marriage has not made it any easier. However, hope keeps her on track. Kaajal would like a paid job, would like to have children, and occasionally fantasises about being a teacher's aide at the local school. She has only been married for seven months. She is determined to wait to have her own children because if she did have them now, without much help, her daily workload could become not just unmanageable but unbearable.

We don't have any plans to have children right now. But maybe in two to three years I will. I would like to have two sons and one daughter. It would be great to have both. First, I want to earn money. I want to build a house and then have children. And if I become financially stable, I just want to help the poor people in the village.

Raju, only child and married at 16: Driven by household's survival

> "Before getting married I dreamed of working in a bank one day. I didn't want to live my life working all day under the sun".

Raju is Kaajal's husband. The story he tells about how he met Kaajal and how they got married does not differ much from his wife's account. However, it is insightful to see early marriage from a male's perspective. Growing up in a poor household and being an only child, there was pressure on Raju to help with farming the family's small plot of land and contributing to the maintenance of the household in any way he could. His mother developed a mental health condition, so there is ongoing stress in the household and the need for extra pairs of hands. Bringing Raju's wife into the family no doubt alleviated the daily burden of survival.

> Kaajal's aunt did not treat her well. So, I told her I would marry her and bring her to my household. My uncle was telling me Kaajal would be good for our household. We married seven months ago, and the wedding festivities lasted for five days. The dowry was minimal because Kaajal's family has no money. So, my family and extended family had to spend Rp 14,000 (USD 140) for the party. We had to sell a few goats. It was a happy time. We were all dancing.

Because marriage and weddings are such vital occasions in Sunsari, even the poorest of families offer parties, and in some cases, they need to sell some assets or even become indebted.

Once the ecstasy of the party is over, though, the reality of the comedown sets in.

> Before marriage, I wanted to go to hang out with friends, I wanted to go out at night, I wanted to spend time with friends day and night. And I could do it. Now, I have to think about it. I have to tell her. I hesitate whether to go and see my friends or not because Kaajal gets tense. We both get tense. I get tense about my family and my wife. We have arguments. She tells me I have to get a job. But I tell her I am not old enough to get a job and it is very difficult to get a job around here.

Raju's parents and uncle, who also live in the household, were not very supportive of Raju finishing high school. They didn't see any point, but more importantly, they needed his young energy and muscles to work the land.

> I used to go to school on occasions only, as my family needed me here most of the time. When I went, I didn't like it. I had missed so much that I could not follow.

What Raju dreamt of before getting married was to work in an office. He fantasised about being able to work indoors in a cool environment, with set start and finish times, and knowing that there would be a regular pay. Now he is realistic and feels this will never happen, so he has another plan. He wants to get a driver's license and perhaps try his luck in India.

> I plan to go abroad and earn some money. If I find a good job, I will stay there. If I earn 35,000 rupees per month (USD 300), I will stay there. I want to live in Nepal, not abroad, but there is no money here. And I have to

learn how to feed my family because one day soon we will have a child.

Raju mentions that if this ever happens, Kaajal may follow him later. But in the meantime, every day starts very early and finishes very late. He gets up at 6 in the morning, releases the cows and goats, and feeds the pigs. He then harvests rice and assists Kaajal with the preparations for breakfast, which is a time of the day when they can be together.

> Around 8 I come and peel potatoes. I cut the potatoes, garlic, onions, and vegetables so that Kaajal can prepare breakfast. Then I go back to the field and come back home for dinner. At night I go fishing. I take a rest there; it is peaceful. Then I go back home to sleep.

Early marriage in Sunsari: New aspirations, old expectations

The cultural and material conditions in poor areas of Sunsari have contributed to early marriage remaining a core trait in the lives of young people. The stories in this chapter suggest the enduring practice of early marriage is fuelled by the disbelief that there are alternatives for these young people. Education is inaccessible and a harsh opportunity cost to helping their families survive. Making a living is very hard. Paid jobs in the area are rare. And so, the prospect of becoming a couple, a family provider, an eloper, a mother, or even a daughter-in-law may provide hopes of new, exciting identities that are well within reach. These prospects also receive community support.

But these days, acceptance and familial pressures surrounding early marriage also clash with young people's evolving sense of autonomy and (sense of) empowerment, facilitated by the expanded imaginaries that mobile phones bring. From stories about making money in India to finding partners through Facebook, or dreaming of pursuing post-high school training to access a paid job, social media has expanded the ways these teenagers think of and experience the transition into adulthood.

Paradoxically, however, in this age of communication and information overload, the accounts of parents, teachers, health workers, and community members consulted for this project confirmed there is very limited communication around the sexual and reproductive lives of young people. They admitted that talking about these topics is embarrassing and that they would avoid the topic where possible, thus leaving teenagers at the onset of their sexuality stripped of information and support. Community members also talked about the high rates of divorce among youth. Huge pressures to make ends meet, abide by in-laws' expectations, or incentives to leave the home to become a migrant worker in India often lead to harsh frictions amongst young couples, including domestic violence. Many community members mentioned that divorces were not common in the past, but they are now, and the older generations have begun to accept them. When they occur, young wives return to their parental home with their offspring, and so will young husbands, who will find it much easier to remarry. These young broken marriages will, in many cases, fuel the cycle of poverty.

Despite the increasing generational gap that is evident in Sunsari, mostly around how technology dominates social networks and aspirations, the incipient cultural change has not rescued young people either from the tight and restrictive social norms that endorse early marital unions or from the poverty that impedes them from joining the world that their mobile phones promise. The dream of a paid job and some access to money for these young Nepalese would help them offer better opportunities to their offspring, more dignity, and some sense of control over their futures.

* * * * *

Extension activities

To extend their learning, students will engage in a variety of activities that encourage them to critically engage with both the local and global dimensions of child marriage and the role of technology in shaping these dynamics.

Extension Activity 1: Students will conduct an analysis of the role of social media in influencing relationships and marriage in Sunsari, comparing this with how social media affects courtship and marriage patterns in another context (e.g., rural India or a community in the Global North). They will explore how technology both challenges and reinforces traditional norms and discuss its impact on young people's perceptions of love, marriage, and gender roles. Students will present their findings and reflect on how social media has become both an enabler and a disruptor in this cultural context.

Extension Activity 2: In small groups, students will create a policy brief proposing a community-based intervention aimed at reducing child marriage in Sunsari. The brief should focus on strategies that address the economic, social, and cultural pressures families face while also empowering young people, especially girls, to make informed choices about their futures. Students will present their policy recommendations, considering the roles of education, family support systems, and local government, as well as potential barriers to implementation.

Extension Activity 3: Students will engage in a creative storytelling activity, using the voices of young brides or brides-to-be. They will write a short narrative or create a multimedia project (e.g., podcast, video) based on interviews or case studies about the experiences of young women in Sunsari. This project will highlight the emotional and social complexities of early marriage, emphasising the tension between familial obligations, personal aspirations, and societal expectations. After presenting their stories, students will discuss the ethical considerations involved in representing the experiences of vulnerable populations and the potential impact of telling such stories.

6
Employment. Independence. (Lack of) Respect: Working as an unskilled youth in Western Sydney, Australia

Learning objectives

By the end of this chapter, students will gain a comprehensive understanding of the challenges faced by youth in Western Sydney, Australia, particularly those school-leavers from low socio-economic backgrounds who are entering the labour market. They will explore the tough working conditions and lack of respect and recognition for young, unskilled workers. Students will critically examine how issues such as the casualisation of work, employer abuse, discrimination, and the high cost of living exacerbate the difficulties these young people face. They will also delve into how the individual realities of this cohort, including mental health challenges, disabilities, gender-diverse identities, or caring responsibilities, often clash with their work lives and aspirations. Students will explore the social and emotional aspects of work, especially the frustration and disillusionment that can arise from systemic barriers to meaningful employment.

* * * * *

History and anthropology have shown us that becoming an adult or beginning to be considered an adult in one's society is not a universal process; neither is there a particular age that indicates the change. The transition is strongly determined by historical, socio-political, and cultural contexts and is often accompanied by a set of responsibilities or allowances that were not part of childhood or early adolescence. Paid work, marriage, sexual activity, the completion of formal education, driving, drinking, or moving out of one's childhood home can signal the end of dependency and the beginning of a new phase of responsibility, thus leading an individual into adulthood.

In wealthy, developed countries, the transition into adulthood is delayed if compared to many places in the Global South. It is often accompanied by the completion of compulsory schooling and may be characterised as a time of opportunity for the middle classes or a time for formally entering the workforce or becoming a parent for working-class youth. In contrast to the constrained options faced by youth in the majority world, where mobility is limited, opportunities scarce, or whether there exist strong cultural imperatives that push novice adults into rigid practices such as early marriage, adolescents finishing high school in developed, cosmopolitan, urban contexts may instead be confronted with a different kind of dilemma: the paradox of choice. Although the narratives around choice may in the end be more rhetorical than real, upon finishing school, many young people in these contexts are able to consider several options around what path their lives will take.

In the bustling urban landscape of Western Sydney, the third largest urban region in Australia, high school leavers from low socioeconomic backgrounds will need to make decisions around what comes next. The myriad subsidised short courses, apprenticeships, and casual job opportunities on offer, added to the fact that many young people remain emotionally, financially, and socially vulnerable, can lead to confusion, instability, and periods of trial and error, and thus a fraught transition into adult life. For youth, schooling, despite all its flaws, provided some sort of structure, routine, and institutional support. Once youth graduate from or leave school, the pressure to succeed and achieve independence, let alone earn some respect and recognition in society, looms large for these young people. As they seek to forge their own paths amid the expectations of their families and peers, many may face individual challenges such as violence at home, undefined gender or sexual identity, physical or mental health problems, or financial constraints. These young people in transition into adulthood may need to fight on several fronts simultaneously.

The stories that follow delve into the experiences of three young people living on the edge of adulthood in Western Sydney as they enter the workforce. Their narratives provide insights into the multifaceted dynamics of youth unemployment or pre-carious work, the defence of one's identity, and the pursuit of fulfilment.

Western Sydney

Greater Western Sydney (GWS) lies within Sydney's metropolitan area. It is a region of around 9,000 km^2, encompassing 14 local government areas, stretching from Windsor in the north to Campbelltown in the south, and from Parramatta in the east to Penrith and the Blue Mountains in the west. GWS stands as a beacon of national significance, driven by its rapid population and economic growth. It houses 47 per cent of Sydney's total population (2.5 million) and produces 31 per cent of Sydney's gross regional product. With about 50 per cent of GWS's population born overseas and the region of choice for about 60 per cent of new arrivals to Australia and residents from over 170 countries, the region is extremely dynamic and culturally diverse. GWS's population is also younger than the rest of the state of New South Wales (NSW), with a median age of 34 compared to the state's median age of 38. However, 42 per cent of GWS's population is below the age of 30. Projections suggest that by 2036, GWS's population will swell to 3 million, absorbing two-thirds of Sydney's overall population growth (Deloitte, Committee for Sydney & Centre for Western Sydney, 2023).

Amid the cultural vibrancy and sustained population growth lies, however, a complex socio-economic landscape characterised by disparities in income, education, and employment. While boasting the third-largest economy in Australia, compared to the other regions of Sydney, GWS grapples with higher unemployment rates, higher rates of crime, a higher average household size, a higher proportion of people living in public or social housing, a higher number of births to teenage mothers, and a significant proportion of children at risk of significant harm and identified as developmentally vulnerable, as well as living in out-of-home care. The region also contends with infrastructural challenges, with transport networks struggling to keep pace with the rapid rate of growth. This leads to congestion and accessibility issues for residents, exacerbating reliance on automobiles and impacting air quality, health, and household budgets (University of Western Sydney and .id Informed Decisions, 2021).

It is in this environment of great contrasts that the stories presented below unfold. The narratives that follow belong to three young people who were interviewed for a project aimed at understanding how young adults in Western Sydney from vulnerable backgrounds (those exposed to poverty, dysfunctional households, violence, or substance abuse) shape their work lives after leaving high school. The research, commissioned by Social Ventures Australia, entailed 22 young people completing a survey and participating in an in-depth interview revolving around the transition to adult life after high school, aspirations and career plans, and work experiences. Participants were aged 17–24 years, did not have or intend to get a university education, and had some experience in the labour market. Half of the participants were born overseas, 40 per cent spoke a language other than English at home, and over a third had left high school early. The sample also included young people who were gender- or sexually diverse and who identified themselves as having an indigenous background. Some participants were single parents or were pregnant at the time. Some of them lived with a disability or dealt with mental health issues. These demographic traits in the sample were reflective of the youth population of GWS's. The three stories presented here were selected based on their powerful narratives, the intersectionality[3] in the identities of the interviewees, and how the themes identified in each generate compelling understandings around the difficulties of transitioning into adult life, especially for those coming from marginalised or disadvantaged backgrounds.

Invisible hurdles: How disability intersects with career aspirations

The first story is about Huang, a determined 21-year-old Chinese-Australian young man with a visual impairment. Huang completed high school with a clear goal: to build a successful career. But his story sheds light on the numerous barriers – both real and perceived – that hinder the career aspirations of young individuals with disabilities. Initially, Huang decided to upskill himself in an area of interest. However, like many others, he discovered that adult education and training often consumes time and financial resources without yielding significant benefits.

In GWS, where hundreds of small, medium, and large adult education providers offer thousands of short courses on all sorts of domains, high school graduates like Huang are enticed by the promise of career advancement through upskilling. As they step into adulthood, they navigate this landscape, hoping that their investment in adult education will lead to a prosperous future.

> When I graduated from High School, I didn't really know what to do. I tried a couple of short courses on counselling

and completed them but then no one would hire me in that area, as I was being told I needed experience, but no one was really willing to take me on for that. So I started volunteering for a health organisation to get the experience and put in the hours. I did give psychology a good try but came to realise that to get an actual paid job in this space is really difficult for me, especially with this barrier of entry because most job applications say you need your driver's license, and I can't do that because I do have the visual impediment…

Huang's aspirations for a career in counselling started to fade as he started to confront the various obstacles that would make that choice quite difficult to realise. Huang remained adaptable and optimistic and started getting into casual employment as a means to support himself, and in the process, he was exposed to alternative career paths.

While I was completing the counselling courses I started working casually in warehousing and operations and stuff like that, just to contribute to the bills. The jobs came through a recruitment agency, which meant I didn't have a boss at the workplace, with whom I could negotiate things such as study time or any special consideration. That's all you find at the start, casual employment, or short-term contracts through recruitment agents.

But Huang really wanted both to get more stable employment and forge a career for himself. His account reveals how challenging and disorienting this stage can be for young people, highlighting the disconnect between employers' expectations and the reality, needs, and aspirations of young adults.

> Employers keep saying, 'we want someone with full-time
> experience', 'we want your full attention', 'we don't want
> you to be working somewhere else'. But they keep you
> as a casual, on-call casual, and they want you to have
> availability for like 20 hours a week, but not being dis-
> tracted with anything else such as study or volunteering
> work. 'So you're basically expecting me to be paid for 20
> hours but have full-time dedication to this position?' It
> was not realistic…

Huang faced significant barriers due to the insistence on specific experience and the inaccessibility of certain workplaces.
His visual impairment and lack of a driver's license compounded
these challenges. While Western Sydney buzzed with opportunities for some, it also yielded frustrations for individuals like
Huang. The lagging development of infrastructure – particularly
limited public transport networks – further restricted the types
of employment he could consider.

> And I applied for many more permanent jobs, but usu-
> ally didn't make it to the interview stage. They always
> said 'we need someone with more experience with this
> system, or this software, … we want you to have expe-
> rience with this particular industry or blah blah…' How
> realistic is that? Plus, with my disability as well … those
> warehouses and distribution centres are really inaccessi-
> ble, in the middle of nowhere, and since I don't have my
> driver's license, it was also more limiting for me.

Huang confronted a deeply personal and obvious barrier when
applying for jobs due to his disability. Even when he reached
the interview stage based solely on his personal merit, he

encountered employers who subtly rejected him, disapproved of his abilities, and doubted whether he could perform the job. This clearly added an emotional toll to a young person who genuinely wanted to embrace adulthood by becoming independent and self-sufficient through employment.

> Sharing my disability is a very personal thing. Even more when you get to the interview stage and want to be transparent and share you have a disability. You're just putting yourself out there when you're already anxious about employment. You have so many things going on, besides a job, you have to support with food and bills and there's so many people that were expecting me to succeed, so going to an interview was very stressful. There was this company once that interviewed me, they make hearing aids, so I thought they would be relatively understanding and accepting of people with disabilities, right? But when I asked them 'Have you ever hired anyone with a disability?', they told me 'no', just like that. And then when I said, 'Oh, well, I do have a vision disability'. Once I said that, everything changed and they weren't interested. They were giving me short answers. They were trying to get me out of the room.

This clearly led to many frustrations for Huang. Despite his honesty, competence for the jobs he was applying for, and willingness to become a responsible worker, he was facing walls on various fronts, impeding him from becoming a self-sufficient adult.

> Some organisations think that I'm unsafe, and that I'm unproductive, and that making adjustments for me will be expensive to the business. And that was a big

challenge for me. And I'm also trying to make employers understand that if they offer me a job, it's not because they're trying to hire someone with a disability so they can meet a quota, but because I am the best person for that job, who also happens to have a disability.

For one of the jobs I had, although I was already doing that job perfectly well, eventually, they fired me. They told me I had to stop because the job was not safe for me, although for over six months, I was one of the best workers and I achieved the same or better results than my other colleagues for that role. And I was completely safe, I had no incidents, I didn't bump into things or had any safety or health issues… I felt humiliated and exploited. And I didn't know where I could go to get support and stuff like that. I felt helpless. And so I was unemployed for a long time, for two years.

Huang's story, however, shows his perseverance and determination to challenge stereotypes and advocate for his worth. The choice of completing more courses was still there, and despite his awareness that training would not necessarily land him a job, it helped him find a potential career path and eventually a workplace where he felt he could bring his full self to work.

I considered studying some courses to make myself a better candidate. I have a slight interest in operations, supply chain management, or being an advisor and consultant for organisations to improve their product and service. But also thought 'what is the point of continuing studying?' I was studying the diploma of logistics, that qualifies me to be a logistics manager, but I was applying for entry-level basic roles, and I had already done those roles. It was a tough time, but I kept on studying the logistics course anyway and kept on applying until I found my current job where I can get by train and bus. So now I'm trying to centre around this career path.

This is a story with a happy ending, and only because Huang was finally noticed by an employer who acknowledged his skills and his commitment and responsibility towards the job. With some minor adjustments to the workplace, such as offering a space in the fridge where he could store his eye drops and adding stair nosing to staircases to help him better navigate the environment, Huang settled into a job.

In my current role we look after the ATM machines for all of Australia. And I am the logistics officer, still a starter job. My current manager is really knowledgeable, and informative. And he really does seem to care about me as a person as well as me as an employee. So you're having that supportive management that understands and wants to promote diversity.

What is important to me now are flexibility and autonomy, so I can do things in my own time, in my own space, of course based on what the company needs. I feel this company is a place where I can really bring my full self to work.

Silenced and overlooked: Employment as a young, unskilled female worker

The second story is told by Rachel, a 19-year-old female whose aspiration after finishing high school was simply to make a living. Coming from a dysfunctional household where she was being pressured to become financially independent, upon finishing high school Rachel was first faced with an abundance of casual jobs in a region where the economy is booming, many businesses are thriving, but where there is a shortage of workers to meet the demand for labour, and where businesses, in pursuit of the highest return, are unwilling to train, protect, or compensate their casual staff fairly. For young female workers like Rachel, with no one to guard for her or help her identify a potential career path, the transition into adulthood in a region like GWS is commonly accompanied by the start of full-time paid work, which can often be an abrupt, violent, and unforgiving experience.

> When I finished school, I went into full time work. I just didn't really had a career in mind and moved around several different jobs. I worked in restaurants, factories, and also at a kids' play centre. I would have liked to stay in that last one but it was a family business and there were family members working there too but I was the one doing all the work, while they were on the phone and doing nothing.

Rachel then moved on to a much more permanent job that offered the benefits of predictable shifts and a more reliable income, and where she was eventually offered the opportunity to manage other workers.

> I moved onto working at a factory, a chicken factory ... The job was putting chickens into trays and packing them. But they were understaffed so I was also doing paperwork and fixing machines. When a co-worker got moved to somewhere else in the factory, I did get

noticed. And then I was put in charge of a lot. But it's not that I was told 'you've done a good job' or 'congratulations', or anything like that…

So Rachel was basically in charge of ensuring the packaging was done following quality standards and also meeting a particular output per hour. She had clearly been assigned some responsibility; however, as a young employee, she felt that responsibility did not bring along with it much respect at all.

> I was the person in charge for all the packing going well, but because of my age, the staff I was supposed to coordinate, chose not to listen. When I had to tell *them* to do something, they tried to tell *me* what to do… Those ladies I was managing were three times my age, so they would turn around and pretty much said to me "stop whinging", when I wanted to tell them what we had to do. They don't want a young person telling them what to do. They want to tell *you* what to do, even though I had more experience in that role, was in charge and I knew what I was doing.

Rachel felt that being young at the workplace was a disadvantage and the root of discrimination, with her co-workers disregarding the authority attached to her job position. She is an adult, employed full time, and responsible for managing others. However, she felt left out, ignored, and thus unable to properly embody adulthood and maturity. Instead, she was being treated as a child.

> I was not being included in decisions or communications when I should have been included. My supervisor had this friend, obviously a lot older than me, and

she was communicating to her all the important things rather than to me … if we had to pack a particular product, rather than coming to me to tell me what I had to do with the rest of the staff, my supervisor would go to her friend, and I would be the last one to know what we were doing.

I did that job for three years. I wanted to quit for a long time because it was unfair … I was not treated well. You don't get treated the same as someone who is older. You feel mistreated because of your age.

As a young, vulnerable woman in need of a regular income, Rachel felt she was being neglected, rejected, and not even guarded in terms of workplace safety.

They never trained me … they just said "do it like this" and sometimes they would say, "we have to cut the hours because you don't know how to do this part of the job well". But they had never trained me in that particular thing. And for the work I was doing you had to be standing for a long period of time on hard ground, in uncomfortable boots, they hurt your feet, and you have to be twisting and turning, constantly repeating the same thing over and over again. In an eight-hour shift you get half an hour break but even with that you wouldn't recover.

Workplaces for young people in this region can therefore be very confronting, and they may need to balance out their need to survive financially with limited skills and qualifications within environments that can be toxic, discriminatory, and even unsafe. In the end, Rachel decided to leave.

> I stayed long in that job because it was only five minutes around the corner and I could get there easily. But I had wanted to quit for a long time because it was unfair. I was in charge of a lot but was not being included and I was not being treated equally. You would have one person like me doing much more work than others, and the others getting away without doing the same amount of work but getting paid the same wage. I just work to earn money for living, and I can put up with the little things, but if it gets too much I have to leave. I also wanted to feel a bit more safe, so I quit.

Rachel then got pregnant. As with many women her age, without clear career aspirations, having a child may provide a sense of achievement, instil them with some societal respect, and fill in an identity void in an environment young adults may find ruthless (Gillies, 2006).

> I am now pregnant. For my next job all I want is just respect and understanding. Especially when I have the kid, I will have more responsibility at home. I will need to work around that. Everyone should be treated equally at work, no matter what your age is. I will be a good worker and committed, as long as they give me that respect.

"No one really wants you there": The workplace through the eyes of transgender youth

The last story belongs to Caylex, a 20-year-old transgender young person who, again, without any real career aspirations or desire to upskill through formal training, dived into adulthood and the world of work while still at high school. References to exploitation and abuse resonate with the previous stories; however, in Caylex's case, the lived experience of being marginalised, even insulted as a non-mainstream individual, leads to a transition into adulthood characterised by societal rejection and constant job-surfing.

> Before I finished high school, I was not necessarily interested in getting into a degree and getting a career through that way. I started off by doing retail work at clothing stores, and McDonald's for a while. I've never really had a good work environment anywhere. As a transgender person half the time you don't even get a job just because you're transgender.
>
> When I go to an interview, if I disclose that I'm transgender, it's almost as if that becomes more of a focus than my actual working abilities. And the stigma around it, and how they're going to have to deal with that is such a problem to them. But they can't say that to you … it's too much effort for them to work around it.

So Caylex spent the first couple of years of adult life trying to survive with whatever job was being offered, even though the work environment could be insulting of Caylex's basic needs, schedules, and even dignity.

> When I worked at a supermarket, they made a big deal that I couldn't use the changerooms, so I had to put all my stuff in the manager's office. And if the manager wasn't in the office, I had to go looking for someone to unlock the office, so I could get my stuff. And that's kind of the same with every kind of place I've worked in so far.

When I worked at McDonald's, I had other staff members making comments, loudly across the entire restaurant with reference to me being transgender … I was thinking "if you have a statement on it, talk to me about it, you don't need to mention it in front of customers and stuff like that". No one wanted me to be there at any point. So I would be put on at the five in the morning shift, alone with one other person, and I was doing everything…

For many of the jobs Caylex was exposed to, the schedules and conditions offered, or the treatment encountered, were in fact a way of being asked to quit.

At one of the jobs they weren't giving me medical time, when I had a full doctor's recommendation that I couldn't do shifts longer than 4 hours due to health issues. But they kept putting me on 10-to-12-hour shifts. I told them I could only do a 4-hour shift at a time. I was happy to work every day for four hours, but they instead just kept putting me on long shifts so they would get mad when I'd call in for that shift and told them I couldn't do it all. So I ended up leaving. And I didn't work for a bit. And then my next job was at a call centre. The environment was almost abusive because you would be told all day "you're going to be fired", "you are going to lose your job" "if you don't get these many things you're going to lose your job". This sent me into almost like a nervous breakdown because I was getting told every day I was going to lose my job even though I was meeting the targets which was calling a set amount of numbers every day. But often people didn't answer, so they would send you home, and then you would only get two hours of pay that entire day, they would blame you for the fact that no one would answer their phone. But if you mention any of this, they tell you "if you don't think this is a good job for you, you shouldn't work here". So I ended up leaving and then it was hard for me to find a job because COVID started happening…

And Caylex then really struggled to find something else but needed to make a living. So everything and anything had to be considered, to the point that Caylex would have to put up with jobs difficult to access by public transport, very poorly paid, and offering unfeasible shifts. Workers such as Caylex struggle to find opportunities to get a job, let alone having some negotiating power to discuss schedules, conditions, or pay.

There are not very many options for me. I had applied to over 250 jobs and hadn't heard anything back. And I needed money to live. And for some of the jobs I got I used to think "I spend all day here. I spend two hours to travel here every day. And then I don't get home till one in the morning sometimes. And then I have to leave again at 7am". There's no point. But then I kind of think "I gotta just suck it up".

They kind of push you into casual contracts. After telling you, "It will be a full-time position, with full time pay", then they tell you "it's full time hours, but you're a casual". So they can get rid of you whenever, basically. For one job I spent three days interviewing … and then training, and you are not paid for that.

Work did not offer much social appeal for Caylex either. No matter the job, Caylex rarely felt welcome, let alone appreciated for the work they completed.

> No one really wants you there. And no one ever really puts that much effort to talk to me. At no point they would be like "Yeah, you did a good job this morning", or ever make a positive comment on your work. But if you are going a little bit slower for five minutes, they would make a comment on that kind of thing. So overall, the environment of the workplaces is kind of negative.

So being young, with limited education, economically disadvantaged, and on top of that transgender, employment in a region like GWS can imply an agonising rite of passage into adulthood. Marginalised, disrespected, ignored, and abused young individuals like Caylex may find work, workplaces, and the people within them hostile and oppressive.

> It's not surprising that many people like me don't stay at a job for more than three months. Half the time shift managers, bosses and stuff, just generally shitty people …. make terrible comments about people like me, and nothing gets done about it, they just abuse you, you are overworked and not paid enough. I've never really had a good work environment anywhere.

A harsh road to maturity

The stories of these three young individuals navigating the first stages of adulthood represent the struggles of many others like them who face a reality slap against the glossy narratives of success and prosperity that a wealthy country like Australia promises to offer. While for a few years high school somewhat shields young people from what happens outside its walls and encourages them to dream big, once they leave, many are pushed to figure out by themselves an unfamiliar set of rules in a hostile environment that, instead of helping them become adults, offers them contempt and neglect. As they attempt to become independent, self-sufficient, emotionally stable, skilled, and responsible, their first steps into the workforce may greet them with scepticism, indifference, and sometimes outright disdain. For those whose identity traits intersect with disability, gender or cultural diversity, single parenthood, or economic or social disadvantage, the workplace can literally become a battle-ground – a place where young people's aspirations and commitment to work are dismissed.

In the eclectic landscape of Western Sydney, where urban and economic growth appear unstoppable and opportunities expansive, young people like Huang, Rachel, and Caylex may find the opposite to be true. The beginning of adulthood and its claim as the start of financial independence and full responsibility may feel like a labyrinth of rejection, limited opportunity, and, sadly, lack of respect. Young workers will need to seek allies – advocates who recognise their worth, employers who invest in their growth, and, importantly, a society that endows them with their dignity.

* * * * *

Extension activities

To deepen their understanding of these issues, students will engage in a variety of extension activities that combine real-world exploration with theoretical analysis.

Extension Activity 1: Students will research the impact of casual work on young employees in Western Sydney and compare this with the employment experiences of youth in other countries or regions (e.g., in the North America, South Asia, or Europe). They will investigate the extent to which the casualisation of work affects mental health, job security, and career progression and then create a presentation that outlines the findings and policy recommendations for improving the conditions of unskilled workers.

Extension Activity 2: In pairs or small groups, students will conduct a case study analysis based on a fictional scenario where a young worker is facing discrimination in the workplace (based on gender, mental health, or disability). Students will analyse the barriers to equality that this worker encounters, propose strategies for workplace inclusion and respect, and discuss how employers, co-workers, and unions can contribute to improving work environments for marginalised employees.

Extension Activity 3: Students will participate in a community engagement project, partnering with a local organisation or advocacy group that supports unskilled youth from dysfunctional families or workers with mental health, disability, or gender-diverse identities. Students will develop a series of workshops or informational materials designed to raise awareness about the challenges faced by these workers, focusing on workers' rights, mental health resources, and strategies for navigating difficult work conditions. Afterward, they will present their findings and experiences to the class, discussing the intersection of work, identity, and well-being.

7
From adversity to hope

Learning objectives

By the end of this final chapter, students will be able to synthesise the key themes from the previous chapters and understand the importance of focusing on an anthropology of hope, which emphasises the strengths, aspirations, and capabilities of young lives and those who care for them, even in the face of significant challenges. Students will critically engage with the idea that, while these young people often experience structural violence through poverty, social inequality, strict social norms, discrimination, and marginalisation, they also possess agency, resilience, and hope for a better future. They will explore how each story, despite the adversity faced by the individuals, reflects a larger narrative of human potential, strength, and a desire for positive change. Students will be encouraged to adopt a perspective that shifts away from deficit-based models of youth to one that centres on the positive trajectories and empowerment of young people. The chapter will underscore how, through an "anthropology of the good" (Robbins, 2013), we can recognise young people's aspirations not just as a reflection of their hardships but as a source of strength that can drive personal and collective transformation.

* * * * *

"In the midst of hate, I found there was, within me, an invincible love. In the midst of tears, I found there was, within me, an invincible smile. And in the midst of winter, I found there was, within me, an invincible summer. And that makes me happy. For it says that no matter how hard the world pushes against me, within me, there's something stronger—something better, pushing right back."

Albert Camus, Return to Tipasa (Retour à Tipasa), 1954

In the introduction to this book, I referred to Katz's (2001) work around establishing connections between different sites, distanced physically but perhaps connected by similar forces that shape the lives of the people within them. Katz transposes the concept of topography from the physical to the social landscape to convey that the physical spaces we inhabit are permeated with sociocultural and power relationships. In the same way topography is used to refer to the physical characteristics of the landscape, the concept is used to appraise intangible traits of landscapes, such as social relationships and power, culture, and everyday life within those sites. Katz introduces the idea of "countertopography" to point at the many forces that shape those social landscapes, usually going unnoticed. Like the hidden geological layers underneath a physical terrain, "countertopography" will disclose the hidden complex relationships that give rise to particular social landscapes and cultural and individual identities.

In the stories of this book, the development of human life is shaped by the **topographies** and **countertopographies** that exist in the specific places where young lives evolve. The stories are connected by topographies of adversity, where infants, children, and youth must push their lives forward against material, cultural, familial, linguistic, educational, geographical, and health obstacles. Each story illustrates, however, how this adversity is mitigated by the support of various individuals and institutions – from close family members to nurses, teachers, and schools. And they reveal that, from the moment of birth — when a human life depends entirely on others for survival, as is the case for the infants in Simeulue in Chapter 2 — to the time when young individuals are expected to fend for themselves, as seen with the teenage spouses in Chapter 5 — the role that carers, communities, and institutions play in protecting or guiding the person changes. These entities may recede, and the intensity of relationships may weaken. The stories of young Western Sydney workers in Chapter 6 reflect the extreme end of this spectrum, where no reference to carers or guarding institutions is found in their narratives. This flow in relationships and systems that support the development of young lives clearly impacts their personhood and identity formation.

In her insightful book *Cross-Cultural Perspectives on Personhood and the Life Course*, anthropologist Cathrine Degnen (2018) fathoms three ways in which personhood – understood by anthropologists as the status of being recognised as a person in any given culture – unfolds in the anthropological literature. The first one is the development of personhood through the exchange of substances (such as food, blood, or genes) and the enactment of practices (such as naming a child or getting married). The second one explores personhood as the result of the relationships between individuals and other entities that are part of the world (animals, the built environment, objects, nature). And the third one focuses on personhood as the result of the interaction with the environment, where "the making of persons and the making of place are part of the same process" (Degnen, 2018, p. 18). These anthropological conceptualisations of personhood resonate in many of the stories in this book: from food exchanges to nurture babies (Chapter 2), to the enactment of the practice of marriage (Chapter 5), to personhood as the result of relationships with other entities (such as with a school setting in Chapter 3), to personhood as the outcome of the interaction with the environment (such as in Chapter 6 where young workers interact with an adverse labour market). Degnen also proposes that the development of personhood needs to be understood beyond Western linear conceptualisations about the life course and that the concept and production of personhood not only vary between cultures but also between different stages of life. This systematic thinking on how personhood is shaped will help the reader appreciate the intersection of the chronological, material, biological, social, and environmental in moulding individualities. It also alludes to how the making of these personhoods in turn creates particular places.

In these final notes, I link the multi-sited stories – connected by similar topographies and **countertopographies** – and highlight the strengths and hopes that emerge in the personhoods of these young individuals, whose lives are shaped by adversity.

Contour lines of hope

The lives of the infants, children, and youth in this book are turbulent, filled with constant obstacles that must be overcome to progress in the path of life. However, as these individuals (or their carers) share their challenges, they also reveal their aspirations, plans, and dreams, and how these dreams are real, possible, and rooted in their own lived places and realities. Anthropologist Appadurai (2013) reminds us that the "capacity to aspire" is humans' unique ability to think of alternative futures and develop strategies to attain them. Anthropologist Haug (2021) builds on this notion to propose a future anthropological stance that expands on hope and "future-making" to propose that by delving into the hopes of individuals in their specific contexts, anthropologists can better understand their struggles, "bringing 'dark' and 'bright' anthropology into dialogue" (p. 73). I see the stories in this book through these lenses, as stories of hope and aspirations, rather than stories of only **structural violence** (Farmer, 2004) and disdain.

In every story, there are strengths that propel young lives forward. Sometimes the strengths that sustain and nurture these young individuals are external relationships, such as when grandmothers in Aceh stay put to support their daughters in birthing and rearing a child, or when women breast-feed the infants of their neighbours. Other times the strengths are internal and shape the character of the individual, such as when five-year-olds show to their parents that they will attend school despite not understanding a single word in the language of instruction, or when a ten-year-old works tirelessly to bring more cash to the household.

Other times, the strengths are built jointly, such as when a married teenage couple develops grit to accept the new and tough reality of the range of responsibilities that come along with married life. And sometimes strengths are built for the benefit of others, such as when transgender or disabled youth confront discriminatory employers, opening a path for future generations to enjoy. In his seminal work, *Development as Freedom,* Amartya Sen (1999) reinvigorated the understanding of human capabilities by prioritising the importance of what individuals **can** actually do, rather than focusing on limited resources or deficits. In his **capabilities approach** he argues that well-being should go beyond traditional metrics like income or wealth and instead consider the capabilities, freedoms, and opportunities individuals have to pursue their aspirations.

Hope has been described as "a temporalized sense of potential, of having a future" (Mar, 2005, p. 365). The strengths and capabilities of the young persons in this book (or of those assisting them to move forward) suggest they envisaged futures and environments where they would be able to flourish, and in most cases those imaginaries were very attainable. When a volunteer nurse in Aceh works towards emphasising the importance of immunisation for babies and toddlers, she firmly believes that it is possible. When immigrant Latin American parents leave everything behind for the sake of better prospects for their children in faraway Australia, they know the obstacle of not speaking the language is temporary and will be overcome. When an orphan 14-year-old maiden works tirelessly in Lombok's tobacco season for some cash, she is convinced that with her pay she will be able to afford gold jewellery, save, and be a provider for her own children one day. When a 16-year-old Nepalese married teenager plans to migrate to India for work, he expects this will help support his young wife and future offspring. And when an employer in Western Sydney embraces employing a young person with a disability, he trusts the young employee can deliver good work. The topographies in this book's stories are also topographies of hope. In particular, because the stories are about infants, children, and youth, hope lives not just in those young individuals, but in those who birth them, feed them, house them, educate them, marry them, and employ them.

Bourdieu (2003) remarks that individuals' practical sense of the future, and the feasible ways in which they can shape that future, are tied to the objective possibilities of their existence. In this sense, each one of the stories suggests that those imageries of more fair, prosperous, or healthy futures, in fact, shape individuals' present actions. In the introduction, the metaphor of **contour lines** (Katz, 2001) was used to refer to how, in the same way contour lines on a map connect points of similar elevation, contour lines can also be imagined as lines connecting distant places related by similar levels of "structural violence". I propose the stories in this book are also, and more importantly, connected by "contour lines of hope", as no matter how monstrous the adversity is, there will be plans, dreams, and aspirations, in the minds of these young individuals and in the ones who care for them. And it is **hope** that will make them resistant to adversity. Be it because of the resilience of their bodies, the courage when living in a language they don't understand, the commitment to help their families survive, the grit shown when forming a new family unit when still very young, or the crave for full financial independence, it is hope and the realisability of that hope that matter.

Hope – together with **value, morality, imagination, well-being, empathy, care, the gift, time, and change** – is a focus of the "anthropology of the good", a term anthropologist Joel Robbins (2013) uses to propose an anthropology that focuses on how human groups in diverse places strive to "create the good in their lives" (p. 457) and which can act as a counterpart to the "anthropology of the suffering". I propose the stories in the book are appraised through the lens of "hope", not just as a unit of anthropological analysis but as a way of promoting dignity for human life anywhere and supporting and respecting their ideals for better futures.

* * * * *

Extension activities

In order to consolidate their learning and engage with the "anthropology of the good", students will participate in a variety of activities that highlight the importance of focusing on hope, resilience, and strength in young people's life experiences.

Extension Activity 1: Students will create a digital collage that represents the hopes, aspirations, and strengths of young people from different backgrounds (drawing on the stories from the chapters). The vision board will include both words and images that reflect the potential for growth, change, and empowerment and will serve as a visual representation of the "anthropology of hope". Students will then present their boards in small groups, explaining the elements they chose and how these aspects connect to the positive trajectories of youth.

Extension Activity 2: In groups, students will design a community empowerment project aimed at fostering the strengths and aspirations of young people in marginalised communities (such as those affected by poverty, child marriage, unemployment, mental health issues, or disability). This project should address the structural challenges young people face while emphasising their capacities for change and self-determination. Students will present their project proposals and discuss how such interventions can build hope and resilience in young people's lives.

Extension Activity 3: Students will write a reflective essay that connects the ideas from the book's chapters, focusing on the resilience and agency of young people. They will analyse how structural violence impacts young people's lives but also explore how these individuals use their strengths to overcome adversity and envision better futures. The essay will emphasise the importance of an "anthropology of the good" as a lens through which to view infants, children, and youth and will conclude by proposing how this perspective can inform policy, activism, and anthropological practice moving forward.

Notes

1. In alignment with the scholarly literature in the critical social sciences that focuses on global inequalities, in this book I use the terms "Global North", "Global South" and "majority world" to refer to the dissimilar global contemporary contexts that are product of colonial histories. The term "Global North" refers to wealthy, industrialised nations primarily located in the Northern Hemisphere, associated with economic and political power. The "Global South" refers to countries, often in the Southern Hemisphere, characterised by lower income and high levels of social inequality. "Majority World" is an alternative and more inclusive term for the Global South, that emphasises that these settings make up the majority of the global population.

2. The dowry system in Nepal has been illegal since 2009. However, the practise is still embedded in many cultural groups in Nepal, and widely practised throughout the country.

3. The concept of intersectionality was coined by Kimberlé Crenshaw (1989), to refer to the way different forms of social stratification, such as race, gender, class, and other axes of identity, intersect to create unique experiences of oppression and privilege.

References

Amigó, M. F. (2010). Small Bodies, Large Contribution: Children's Work in the Tobacco Plantations of Lombok, Indonesia. *The Asia Pacific Journal of Anthropology*, 11(1), pp. 34–51.

Amigó, M.F. (2012). Liminal but competent: Latin American migrant children and school in Australia. *Child Studies in Asia-Pacific Contexts*, 2(1), pp.61–75.

Amigó, M.F. (2017). Confronting school: Immigrant families, hope, education. *Diaspora, Indigenous, and Minority Education*, *11*(3), pp.148–161.

Amigó, M. F. and Gurung, S. (2021). The Transformational Possibilities of a Peer Education Program to Address Child Marriage in Nepal. *Development in Practice*, 32(7), pp. 890–900. doi: 10.1080/09614524.2021.1937572

Amigó, M. F., García Palacios, M., Enriz, N. and Hecht, A. C. (2022). Indigenous Epistemologies of Childhood in Contexts of Inequality: Three Case Studies from the "Global South. *Childhood*, 29(3), pp. 307–321.

Appadurai, A. (2013). *The Future as Cultural Fact: Essays on the Global Condition*. London: Verso.

Ayuningtyas, B., Prabowo, S. M., Sari, Y. and Wijaya, N. R. (2022). Stunting and its Determinants in Aceh: A Comprehensive Review. *Journal of Public Health Research*, 11(2), pp. 150–160.

Australian Institute of Health and Welfare (2024). Children's headline indicators. Available at: https://www.aihw.gov.au/ [Accessed 16 December 2024].

Behar, R. (1996). *The Vulnerable Observer: Anthropology That Breaks Your Heart*. Boston: Beacon Press.

Bourdieu, P. (2003). *Méditations pascaliennes* [1997]. Paris: Éditions du Seuil.

Cannella, G. S., & Viruru, R. (2004). *Childhood and postcolonization: Power, education and contemporary practice.* New York: RoutledgeFalmer.

Cederroth, S. and Gerdin, I. (1986). Cultivating poverty: The case of the Green Revolution in Lombok. In: I. Nørlund, S. Cederroth, I. and Gerdin. eds., *Rice Societies: Asian Problems and Prospects.* London: Curzon Press pp. 124–150.

Cregan, K., & Cuthbert, D. (Eds.). (2014). *Global childhoods: Issues and debates.* London: Sage Publications.

Crenshaw, K. (1989). Demarginalizing the Intersection of Race and Sex: A Black Feminist Critique of Antidiscrimination Doctrine, Feminist Theory and Antiracist Politics. *University of Chicago Legal Forum*, 1989(1), pp. 139–167.

Das, V. (2007). *Life and Words: Violence and the Descent into the Ordinary.* Berkeley: University of California Press.

de Certeau, M. (1980). *L'invention du quotidien: 1. Arts de faire.* Paris: Éditions Gallimard.

Degnen, C. ed. (2018). *Cross-cultural Perspectives on Personhood and the Life Course* (New York: Routledge).

Deloitte, Committee for Sydney & Centre for Western Sydney (2023). Western Sydney: Progress and prospects. Available at: https://www.westernsydney.edu.au/content/dam/digital/images/centre-for-western-sydney/WesternSydneyProgressandProspects.pdf [Accessed 13 December 2024].

Farmer, P. (2004). An Anthropology of Structural Violence. *Current Anthropology*, 45(3), pp. 305–325.

Gillies, V. (2006). *Marginalised Mothers: Exploring Working Class Experiences of Parenting.* 1st ed. Routledge. Available at: https://doi.org/10.4324/9780203966792.

Gonzalez, A. (2019). Commercial Determinants of Health: A Systematic Review of the Literature. *BMC Public Health*, 19(1), 900.

Guragain, A. M., Paudel, B. K., Lim, A. and Choonpradub, C. (2017). Adolescent Marriage in Nepal: A Subregional Level Analysis. *Marriage & Family Review*, 53(4), pp. 307–319.

Hage, G. (2003). *Against Paranoid Nationalism: Searching for Hope in a Shrinking Society*. Annandale: Pluto Press.

Haug, M. (2020) 'Framing the future through the lens of hope', *Zeitschrift für Ethnologie (ZfE) / Journal of Social and Cultural Anthropology (JSCA)*, 145(1), pp. 71–92.

Hofer, A. (2020). Young People's Perceptions of Marriage in Rural Nepal. *The Asia Pacific Journal of Anthropology*, 21(2), pp. 117–133. doi: 10.1080/14442213.2020.1716318

Jensen, R. and Thornton, R. (2003). Early Female Marriage in the Developing World. *Gender & Development*, 11(2), pp. 9–19. doi: 10.1080/741954311

Katz, C. (2001). On the Grounds of Globalization: A Topography for Feminist Political Engagement. *Signs*, 26(4), pp. 1213–1234.

Kirchheiner, O. (2016). *Culture and Christianity negotiated in Hindu society: A case study of a church in central and western Nepal*. PhD thesis. Middlesex University / Oxford Centre for Mission Studies (OCMS) School of Law.

Lancy, D. F. (2008). *The Anthropology of Childhood: Cherubs, Chattel, Changelings*. 2nd ed. Cambridge: Cambridge University Press.

LeVine, R. A. and New, R. S. eds. (2008). *Anthropology and Child Development: A Cross-Cultural Reader*. 1st ed. Carlton: Blackwell Publishing.

Liebel, M., 2020. *Decolonizing childhoods: From exclusion to dignity*. Bristol: Policy Press.

Mar, P. (2005). Unsettling Potentialities: Topographies of Hope in Transnational Migration. *Journal of Intercultural Studies*, 26(4), pp. 361–378.

Montgomery, H. (2009). *An Introduction to Childhood: Anthropological Perspectives on Children's Lives*. Chichester: Wiley-Blackwell.

MWCSW (Ministry of Women, Children and Social Welfare) (2016). *National Strategy to End Child Marriage in Nepal*. Kathmandu: Ministry of Women, Children and Social Welfare.

NSW Department of Education (2021). Schools: Language diversity in NSW, 2020. Available at: https://www.education.nsw.gov.au/ [Accessed 16 December 2024].

OECD/ADB (2015), Education in Indonesia: Rising to the Challenge, Reviews of National Policies for Education, OECD Publishing, Paris, https://doi.org/10.1787/9789264230750-en.

Randell, M., Li, M., Rachmi, C. N. et al. (2024). Of the Community but not of the Health System: Translating Community Health Workers' Knowledge into Credible Advice in Aceh, Indonesia. *Discover Health Systems*, 3, p. 5.

Rai, R.K. (2018). Changes in Marriage and Kinship Systems among Bantawa Rai in Eastern Nepal. In: Proceedings of the International Conference on Social Structure and Social Change, November 21–22, 2017, Pokhara. Lalitpur: Nepal Sociological Association, pp. 133–143.

Regmi, P. R., van Teijlingen, E., Silwal, R. C. and Dhital, R. (2022). Role of Social Media for Sexual Communication and Sexual Behaviors: A Focus Group Study among Young People in Nepal. *Journal of Health Promotion*, 10, pp. 153–166. Available at: https://doi.org/10.3126/jhp.v10i1.50995 [Accessed 16 July 2024].

Robbins, J. (2013). Beyond the Suffering Subject: Toward an Anthropology of the Good. *Journal of the Royal Anthropological Institute*, 19(3), pp. 447–462. doi: 10.1111/1467-9655.12040

Richards, E. (2008). *Destination Australia: Migration to Australia Since 1901*. Sydney: UNSW Press.

Sen, A. (1999). *Development as Freedom*. New York: Knopf.

Stephens, S. (1995). *Children and the Politics of Culture*. Princeton: Princeton University Press.

Sunam, R. (2015). The significance of foreign labour migration and land for poverty reduction in Nepal. In: A. Heshmati, E. Maasoumi, and G. Wan, eds. *Poverty Reduction Policies and Practices in Developing Asia: Economic Studies in Inequality, Social Exclusion and Well-Being*. Singapore: Springer. doi:10.1007/978-981-287-420-7_12

UNICEF (2019). Nepal among top 10 countries for prevalence of child marriage among boys. UNICEF [press release], 7 June. Available at: https://www.unicef.org/press-releases/nepal-among-top-10-countries-prevalence-child-marriage-among-boys [Accessed 16 July 2024].

UNICEF (2022). Child marriage in South Asia. Available at: https://data.unicef.org/topic/child-protection/child-marriage/ [Accessed 16 July 2024].

University of Western Sydney and .id Informed Decisions, 2021. *Western Sydney (LGA) 2021 Census Results*. Comparison year: 2016, Benchmark area: Greater Sydney. [pdf] Available at: https://profile.id.com.au/cws/about-profile-id [Accessed 24 May 2024].

Valle, M. (2016). *Desbordamiento y Resistencia*. Mexico City: Universidad Autónoma de Puebla.

Van der Kraan, A. (1980). Lombok: *Conquest, Colonization and Underdevelopment*. Singapore: Heinemann Educational Books, Asian Studies Association of Australia Publication Series.

Van Maanen, J. (2011). *Tales of the Field: On Writing Ethnography*. 2nd ed. Chicago: University of Chicago Press.

Vandenbroeck, M., Roets, G. and Snoeck, A. (2009). Immigrant Mothers Crossing Borders: Nomadic Identities and Multiple Belongings in Early Childhood Education. *European Early Childhood Education Research Journal*, 17(2), pp. 203–216.

Index